D0040791

Farm Journal's Choice Chocolate Recipes

Other cookbooks by FARM JOURNAL

FARM JOURNAL'S COUNTRY COOKBOOK

FARM JOURNAL'S COMPLETE PIE COOKBOOK

LET'S START TO COOK

HOMEMADE BREAD

AMERICA'S BEST VEGETABLE RECIPES

HOMEMADE CANDY

HOMEMADE COOKIES

HOMEMADE ICE CREAM AND CAKE

FAMILY FAVORITES FROM COUNTRY KITCHENS

THE THRIFTY COOK

COUNTRY FAIR COOKBOOK

GREAT HOME COOKING IN AMERICA

FARM JOURNAL'S HOMEMADE SNACKS

FARM JOURNAL'S BEST-EVER RECIPES

FARM JOURNAL'S GREAT DISHES FROM THE OVEN

FARM JOURNAL'S FREEZING AND CANNING COOKBOOK

FARM JOURNAL'S FRIENDLY FOOD GIFTS FROM YOUR KITCHEN

Farm Journal's Choice Chocolate Recipes

By Elise W. Manning
Farm Journal Food Editor

Recipes selected and edited
By Patricia A. Ward
Assistant Food Editor

FARM JOURNAL, INC.
Philadelphia, Pennsylvania

Distributed to the trade by
DOUBLEDAY COMPANY, INC., Garden City, New York

Book design and drawings
By Maureen Sweeney
Farm Journal Art Staff

Photography supervised
By Alfred Casciato
Farm Journal Associate Art Director

Copyright © 1978 by Farm Journal, Inc.
All rights reserved
Printed in the United States of America

ISBN: 0-385-14777-5

Library of Congress Catalog Card Number 78-59323

Second Printing

Contents

Chapter

1	All About Chocolate	7
	Chocolate Through the Centuries	8
	The Cacao Tree and Bean	9
	The Manufacture of Cocoa and Chocolate from the Cacao Bean	11
	The Different Types of Chocolate Products	12
	Tips on Cooking with Chocolate	13
2	Plain and Fancy Cakes	15
3	All Kinds of Cookies	75
4	Batches of Brownies	101
5	A Potpourri of Pies	129
6	Downright Delicious Desserts and Sauces	157
7	Fudge and More Fudge	185
8	Mmm! What Good Candy!	201
	INDEX	217

COLOR PHOTOGRAPHS

Five Candies for Gift-giving   facing page 64

Chocolate Cheese Pie

Chocolate-Lemon Cake and Southern Pound Cake

A Potpourri of Chocolate Favorites

More Chocolate Specialties   facing page 160

Three Chocolate Treats

Elegant Chocolate Log

Chocolate Charlotte Russe

Color photographs by: William Hazzard/Hazzard Studios, Hoedt Studios and Mel Richman Studios.

All About Chocolate

Right after our biggest blizzard last winter, we received an avalanche of chocolate recipes from the farms and ranches of our Farm Journal magazine readers—more than 10,000 recipes in all.

This staggering amount of mail came in response to a request for our readers' chocolate recipes. Not only did we receive favorite recipes in every category from cakes to fudge, but we also found that chocolate rates as "tops" with many of our readers.

"Are you planning to publish a book on chocolate?" many asked. We really weren't, but these recipes convinced us that we should; they were too good to resist.

And so, for the next several months, the rich aroma of chocolate drifted through our halls as we tested and tasted chocolate recipes in our Farm Journal kitchens. Of the original 10,000, we have selected the ones we consider the very best just for you.

When they sent their recipes, many of our contributors also told us why these confections were such special favorites in their families. We enjoyed these comments so much that we are printing many of them right along with the recipes.

Chocolate Through the Centuries

The story of chocolate as we know it dates back to the discovery of America in 1492. Christopher Columbus returned to Spain from his voyage to the New World and presented his newly found treasures to King Ferdinand V. One of the treasures was a small pile of dark brown almond-shaped beans. They were cacao beans, the source of all chocolate and cocoa. The King was not impressed. Little did he know the potential fortune he held in the palm of his hand.

However, in 1519, the Spanish explorer, Hernando Cortez, first saw the bean and became aware of its commercial possibilities.

During his conquest of Mexico, Cortez was invited to a banquet by Montezuma and one of the delicacies of the evening was a thick, cold, unsweetened beverage served in golden goblets. It was called *chocolatl*. Cortez began to observe the Aztec's methods of cultivating the cacao bean and he decided this might prove to be a new source of revenue. He watched the Indians roast and grind the beans and flavor them with vanilla, peppers, herbs and spices. While sailing home to Spain, he was convinced that the *chocolatl* could become a luxurious delicacy. He also knew that it was too bitter for Spanish tastes. Over the years, the Spaniards learned to sweeten the drink with cane sugar and serve it hot.

The new drink became an instant hit among Spanish aristocracy. So Spain decided to plant the cacao in its overseas colonies and cacao soon became a very profitable business. The Spaniards managed to keep the art of cultivation of the cacao bean and the preparation of the drinking chocolate a secret from the rest of Europe for almost one hundred years.

As Spain declined in power, the secret of cacao leaked out and Spain's monopoly of the chocolate trade was over.

By the middle of the 1600s, chocolate was *the* drink at the fashionable court of France. And the English began cultivating cacao in the British West Indies. In 1657, the first of many famous English chocolate houses appeared in London.

The invention of the cocoa press in 1828 reduced chocolate prices drastically and at the same time improved the quality of the product. The press was able to squeeze out part of the cocoa butter, which produced a chocolate with a smoother consistency and a more pleasing flavor.

Chocolate was brought to the American colonies by traders who sailed to the West Indies and South America. The first chocolate factory in this country was established in New England in 1765.

Early in the 19th century the two biggest developments took place in the history of chocolate. First of all, in 1876, Daniel Peter of Switzerland invented a way of making milk chocolate for eating by combining milk and chocolate. It was another Swiss who invented the process of "conching"—a process by which the chocolate is kneaded into a smooth, velvety texture. This was a vast improvement as up until the conching method was perfected, all chocolate was coarsely grained.

Chocolate is as American as apple pie and hot dogs. In fact, during World War II, our government realized how important a little piece of chocolate was to our soldiers' morale. It allocated shipping space for the importation of the cacao bean so that the GI could have his beloved chocolate bar as part of his rations.

The Cacao Tree and Bean

The origin of the cacao tree is still a mystery. Some say it originated in Brazil, others insist it was Venezuela and still others are sure it was native to Central America.

But one thing we do know is that the cacao tree is definitely a tropical plant and thrives only in hot rainy climates. So this means that the cultivation of the tree is confined to lands that are no more than 20 degrees north or south of the equator. The cacao tree grows in many countries in Central and South America and is especially prolific along the West Coast of Africa.

The cacao tree is unique in that its flowers and fruit (the pods) cluster on both the trunk and the branches. The tree is very sensitive to wind and hot sun especially during the first two to four years. Therefore, it must be grown in valleys where it can be sheltered from the wind and the sun by larger shade trees.

The trees bloom and bear fruit in five years, though some will produce fruit in three or four years. The tiny pink, white or yellow blossoms are odorless, and the ripened pods resemble little footballs. Each pod contains 20 to 40 cacao beans.

The job of harvesting the ripe cacao pods is not easy. The trees are so fragile that harvesters can't climb the tree to reach the higher branches, so they use a "cacao hook," which is a knife attached to the end of a long pole. Cutlasses are used to whack the pods on the lower branches. Next, the harvesters break open the pods with a machete. A good worker can open 500 pods in an hour. Then the ivory-colored beans are scooped out of the pod.

The beans change color from ivory to purple after they are exposed to the air. Then they are placed in boxes to ferment. This takes from two to nine days, depending on the humidity.

The fermenting of the pulp and the curing action that takes place inside the bean are what produce the first whiff of the chocolate aroma. Now the beans have turned a rich brown.

The beans are dried on trays or bamboo matting, in the sun or indoors by hot air pipes. The dried beans are poured into large sacks stamped with the plantation owner's name. Each sack holds about 200 pounds of beans. They are ready to be sent to shipping centers where they will be transported to cocoa and chocolate factories all over the world.

The Manufacture of Cocoa and Chocolate from the Cacao Bean

The sacks of cacao beans are opened at the chocolate factory and carefully inspected for quality and then cleaned thoroughly.

Next, the beans are roasted in rotating machines at very high temperatures to bring out the distinctive chocolate aroma. The roasting process lasts from 30 minutes to two hours, depending on the variety and condition of the particular bean. During the process, a skilled supervisor periodically takes samples to assure a uniform quality of roast. When the beans are properly roasted, they are cooled quickly and their thin shells are removed by a "cracker and fanner." The remaining meat of the bean, called the nib, is ground between heavy steel discs. During the grinding process, the heat releases the cocoa butter in the nibs, forming a semi-liquid paste, known as the chocolate flavor liquor. This semi-liquid paste is then poured into molds and allowed to cool until hard. The resulting cakes are familiar to every homemaker. They are unsweetened or bitter chocolate.

To make cocoa powder, the chocolate liquor is melted and placed in a hydraulic press. Chocolate liquor contains about 50% cocoa butter. Part of this cocoa butter is squeezed out under tremendous pressure. The remaining hard mass, known as "cocoa cake," is ground into a fine powder. This is packaged and sold in supermarkets as ordinary cocoa or "breakfast cocoa." "Ready to serve" or "sweet milk cocoa" is a combination of cocoa powder, sugar and milk.

Milk chocolate is made by adding sugar, cocoa butter and milk solids to the chocolate liquor according to standard formulas. This liquid mixture is then formed into the familiar bars, patties, Easter bunnies, etc.

The Different Types of Chocolate Products

Unsweetened chocolate or baking chocolate is the basic chocolate from which all other products are made. It's pure "chocolate liquor" molded into 1-ounce blocks which are packed eight to a carton. Used for all kinds of baking.

Semisweet chocolate is unsweetened chocolate blended with sugar, additional cocoa butter and flavorings. It's also molded into 1-ounce blocks and packed eight to a carton. Used in baking, too.

Semisweet chocolate pieces, also called bits or chips, are a blend of unsweetened chocolate, sugar and cocoa butter, specially formulated to hold their shape softly when baked.

Sweet cooking chocolate is similar to semisweet chocolate, but it contains a higher proportion of sugar. Packaged in 4-ounce bars and used in baking. Also called German sweet chocolate.

Liquid or premelted baking chocolate is an unsweetened liquid product with a cocoa base packaged in 1-ounce packets. It is used in place of melted unsweetened chocolate in baking.

Milk chocolate is sweet chocolate with milk added and comes in the familiar candy bar.

Chocolate syrup is a combination of cocoa, sugar, corn syrup and flavoring. It is used in baking, beverages and as an ice cream topping. Available in 5½- and 16-ounce cans.

Milk chocolate fudge topping is like chocolate syrup, but has added milk, cream or butter. It is used only as a dessert topping.

12

Baking cocoa is unsweetened chocolate with varying amounts of cocoa butter removed. Regular cocoa contains about 16% cocoa butter. Dutch processed cocoa with about the same cocoa butter content has been treated with an alkali and has a stronger flavor and darker color. It's used in baking and making beverages.

Instant cocoa is a blend of cocoa, sugar and other flavorings. It is used in beverages because it dissolves quickly. This should not be used in a recipe that requires baking cocoa unless the recipe specifies "instant cocoa."

Chocolate substitutes, such as chocolate-flavored chips, do not contain chocolate liquor. They have a cocoa base to which vegetable fats are added. So even though they are flavored to taste like chocolate, they technically are not.

White chocolate—this is called "the chocolate that isn't." The cacao mass which gives chocolate it's distinctive brown color and deep flavor does not go into white chocolate. Because of the absence of chocolate liquor, it doesn't meet the United States Food and Drug Administration standards for chocolate manufacture. It may be made with vegetable fats instead of cocoa butter and tinted with vegetable coloring and it contains added flavors.

Tips on Cooking with Chocolate

Melting chocolate

Chocolate scorches easily, so always melt it over hot—not boiling—water. It is best to use a double boiler, but you can improvise by using a cup or bowl in a small saucepan over very gentle heat. The water must be kept below simmering to prevent steam from curling up and hitting the chocolate. If steams gets into the melted chocolate it will immediately thicken the mixture to a stiff mass. If this does happen, however, you can rescue the chocolate by softening it again. To do this, add 1 to 2 tablespoons of vegetable shortening (never use butter as it contains moisture which will cause the chocolate to stiffen even more!) to the chocolate and stir vigorously.

You can also melt chocolate directly over very low heat in a heavy gauge saucepan, but you must watch the mixture carefully.

How to make chocolate curls

Use a vegetable peeler with a long narrow blade and a chunk or bar of chocolate. Warm chocolate and blade slightly. Be sure your peeler is absolutely dry. Draw the peeler along the smooth surface of the chocolate.

How to grate chocolate

Be sure that the block of chocolate is cool and firm. Grate on hand grater, cleaning the grater often so that the chocolate doesn't clog the surface of blade. You can use a blender, but be sure to cut the chocolate in small pieces first.

How to store chocolate

Chocolate should be stored in a cool, dry place at a temperature of about 60° F. If the chocolate becomes too warm, the cocoa butter rises to the surface and forms a dusty gray film known as "bloom." This "bloom" is not harmful and, once the chocolate is melted, it returns to its natural rich brown color.

If you do store chocolate in the refrigerator or freezer, take it out and let it stand until it returns to room temperature before you use it in a recipe. Chocolate is very sensitive to sudden changes of temperature and you will not get the best results if you do not treat it with respect.

Plain and Fancy Cakes

A thousand cake recipes were submitted by farm women as their top choice chocolate recipes. From these recipes, we selected and tested the collection in this chapter. There's a cake for every occasion.

You'll find lots of great snacking cakes—the kind that bake in a big 13x9x2-inch pan and require no frosting or have their own bake-on crunchy topping. Kids like them for lunch box treats, and men like them to eat in the field.

There are some excellent grass-roots recipes that swept through the country during World War II, such as the Victory Chocolate Cake and the Mayonnaise Chocolate Cake. These cakes were developed to use less sugar and no butter, which were rationed during the war and used sparingly by homemakers.

Featured too, are what we call "surprise" cakes. . .Red Beet Chocolate Cake, Chocolate Zucchini Cake, Chocolate Sauerkraut Cake and Pumpkin Chocolate Cake. Farm women make these to use up surplus garden vegetables, and they are delicious! The vegetables make them extra moist and nutritious.

15

SPICED CHOCOLATE/APPLESAUCE CAKE

Good old-fashioned applesauce cake has always been a favorite—especially with men. And, when you add cocoa, it becomes extra special. Serve it plain with a dusting of sugar or spread lavishly with the fluffy frosting.

2½ c. sifted flour	2 eggs
½ c. baking cocoa	1 tsp. vanilla
2 tsp. baking soda	1 c. applesauce
1 tsp. ground cinnamon	1 c. buttermilk
1 tsp. salt	⅓ c. boiling water
¾ c. shortening	Chocolate Fluff Frosting .
2 c. sugar	(recipe follows)

Sift together flour, cocoa, baking soda, cinnamon and salt; set aside.

Cream together shortening and sugar in mixing bowl until light and fluffy, using electric mixer at medium speed. Add eggs, one at a time, beating well after each addition. Blend in vanilla and applesauce.

Add dry ingredients alternately with buttermilk to creamed mixture, beating well after each addition. Beat in boiling water. (Batter is thick.) Pour batter into greased and waxed paper-lined 13x9x2" baking pan.

Bake in 350° oven 1 hour or until cake tests done. Cool 10 minutes in pan on rack. Remove from pan; cool on rack. When cake is cooled, spread with Chocolate Fluff Frosting. Cut in squares. Makes 16 servings.

Chocolate Fluff Frosting: Melt 2 (1 oz.) squares unsweetened chocolate over hot water. Cool to room temperature. Blend together ½ c. sifted confectioners sugar, ¼ c. soft butter or regular margarine, melted chocolate and 1 tsp. vanilla in bowl until smooth. Beat 2 egg whites in another bowl until soft peaks form, using electric mixer at high speed. Gradually beat in 1 c. sifted confectioners sugar, 2 tblsp. at a time, until egg white mixture is glossy and stiff. Fold chocolate mixture into egg white mixture.

AUNT GEORGIE'S CHOCOLATE CAKE

"Chocolate is first choice in our house," writes a North Dakota woman. "And this one-bowl cake is a real time-saver. Sometimes I substitute plain yogurt for the sour milk—makes it extra fluffy and moist. No need to frost. Serve warm from the oven with a glass of cold milk."

1½ c. sifted flour
1 c. sugar
3 tblsp. baking cocoa
1 tsp. baking soda
½ tsp. salt
1 egg
¼ c. butter or regular
   margarine, melted

1 c. sour milk*
¼ c. hot water
1 tsp. vanilla
Sifted confectioners
   sugar

Sift together flour, sugar, cocoa, baking soda and salt into mixing bowl. Add egg, butter, sour milk, hot water and vanilla. Beat with electric mixer at medium speed 2 minutes. Pour batter into greased 13x9x2" baking pan.

17

Bake in 350° oven 20 minutes or until cake tests done. Cool in pan on rack. Dust with confectioners sugar. Cut in squares. Makes 16 servings.

*Note: To sour milk, place 1 tblsp. vinegar in measuring cup. Add enough milk to make 1 c.

WEST HAVEN CHOCOLATE CAKE

A lovely light chocolate colored and flavored cake. Very subtle flavor of dates throughout the cake. Cut in big squares and top with a scoop of vanilla ice cream.

8 oz. pitted dates, chopped
1 tsp. baking soda
1 c. boiling water
1¾ c. sifted flour
2 tblsp. baking cocoa
½ tsp. salt

1 c. shortening
1 c. sugar
2 eggs
1 (6 oz.) pkg. semisweet chocolate pieces
½ c. chopped walnuts

Combine dates, baking soda and boiling water in small bowl. Cool to room temperature.

Sift together flour, cocoa and salt; set aside.

Cream together shortening and sugar in mixing bowl until light and fluffy, using electric mixer at medium speed. Add eggs, one at a time, beating well after each addition.

Blend in date mixture. Then stir in dry ingredients. Pour into greased 13x9x2" baking pan. Sprinkle with chocolate pieces and walnuts.

Bake in 350° oven 35 minutes or until cake tests done. Cool in pan on rack. Cut in squares. Makes 16 servings.

MOUTH-WATERING CHOCOLATE CAKE

"Everyone in our family is a chocolate freak," a Missouri woman told us, "but we all agree this cake is our special chocolate recipe. My husband prefers a rich butter cream icing to a chocolate one."

2¼ c. sifted cake flour
2 tsp. baking soda
½ tsp. salt
½ c. butter or regular margarine
2¼ c. brown sugar, packed
3 eggs

1½ tsp. vanilla
3 (1 oz.) squares unsweetened chocolate, melted and cooled
1 c. dairy sour cream
1 c. boiling water
Butter Cream Frosting (recipe follows)

Sift together cake flour, baking soda and salt; set aside.

Cream together butter and brown sugar in mixing bowl until light and fluffy, using electric mixer at medium speed. Add eggs, one at a time, beating well after each additon. Beat in vanilla and chocolate.

Add dry ingredients alternately with sour cream to creamed mixture, beating well after each addition. Stir in boiling water. (Batter is very thin.) Pour batter into greased 13x9x2" baking pan.

Bake in 350° oven 35 minutes or until cake tests done. Cool in pan on rack. Frost with Butter Cream Frosting. Cut in squares. Makes 16 servings.

Butter Cream Frosting: Sift 1 (1 lb.) box confectioners sugar into mixing bowl. Add ½ c. soft butter or regular margarine, 1 tsp. vanilla and 2 to 3 tblsp. hot water. Beat until smooth.

VICTORY CHOCOLATE CAKE

"This cake was very popular during the second World War when I was a new bride," wrote a Minnesota woman. "Sugar was rationed and very precious. This recipe uses very little sugar. It is still our nicest chocolate cake and all my friends beg for the recipe."

2 c. sifted flour	⅓ c. sugar
½ c. baking cocoa	1½ c. dark corn syrup
2¼ tsp. baking soda	3 eggs, separated
¾ tsp. salt	1½ tsp. vanilla
¾ c. shortening	1 c. cooled coffee

Sift together flour, cocoa, baking soda and salt; set aside.

Cream together shortening and sugar in mixing bowl until light and fluffy, using electric mixer at medium speed. Blend in corn syrup and egg yolks. Beat in vanilla.

Add dry ingredients alternately with coffee to creamed mixture, beating well after each addition.

Beat egg whites in another bowl until stiff peaks form. Fold egg whites into cake batter. Pour batter into greased 13x9x2" baking pan.

Bake in 350° oven 45 minutes or until cake tests done. Cool in pan on rack. Frost as desired. Cut in squares. Makes 16 servings.

OUTSTANDING CHOCOLATE CAKE

A 30-year-old recipe from Illinois that our Farm Journal tasting staff rated "fantastic." Tender crumbed, deep chocolate flavor, with an ultra creamy frosting that tastes like chocolate whipped cream.

2 c. sifted cake flour
½ tsp. baking powder
⅛ tsp. salt
½ c. butter or regular
 margarine
1½ c. sugar
2 eggs
1 tsp. vanilla

2 (1 oz.) squares
 unsweetened chocolate,
 melted and cooled
1 tsp. baking soda
1 c. iced water
Whipped Chocolate Frosting
 (recipe follows)

Sift together cake flour, baking powder and salt; set aside.

Cream together butter and sugar in mixing bowl until light and fluffy, using electric mixer at medium speed. Add eggs, one at a time, beating well after each addition. Blend in vanilla and cooled chocolate, mixing well.

Combine baking soda and iced water; stir until baking soda is dissolved. Add dry ingredients alternately with iced water mixture to creamed mixture, beating well after each addition. Pour batter into greased 13x9x2" baking pan.

Bake in 350° oven 35 minutes or until cake tests done. Cool in pan on rack 10 minutes. Remove from pan; cool on rack. Frost sides and top of cake with Whipped Chocolate Frosting. Cut in squares. Makes 16 servings.

Whipped Chocolate Frosting: Combine 2 (1 oz.) squares unsweetened chocolate and 2 tblsp. butter or regular margarine in small saucepan. Heat over low heat until chocolate and butter are melted. Cool slightly. Combine cooled chocolate mixture, 1 c. sifted confectioners sugar, 1 egg, ⅛ tsp. salt, ¼ c. milk and 1 tsp. vanilla in metal mixing bowl. Set bowl in another bowl filled with ice cubes and water. Beat with electric mixer at high speed until mixture becomes light and fluffy and forms soft peaks, about 5 minutes.

21

WHOLE WHEAT CHOCOLATE CAKE

Starting with her aunt's favorite chocolate cake recipe, an Alabama woman substituted whole wheat flour for some of the white flour, reduced the sugar and salt and came up with this sturdy, fudgy cake. This cake tastes a bit different but is delicious.

1½ c. sugar
1 c. sifted flour
¾ c. stirred whole wheat
    flour
2 tsp. baking soda
1 tsp. salt
1 c. butter or regular
    margarine

1 c. water
¼ c. baking cocoa
2 eggs, beaten
½ c. dairy sour cream
Cocoa Frosting (recipe
    follows)

Stir together sugar, flour, whole wheat flour, baking soda and salt in mixing bowl.

Combine butter, water and cocoa in saucepan. Bring mixture to a boil, stirring constantly. Remove from heat. Pour into flour mixture. Mix well, using spoon. Blend in eggs and sour cream, mixing well. Pour batter in greased 13x9x2" baking pan.

Bake in 375° oven 30 minutes or until cake tests done. Cool in pan on rack. Meanwhile, prepare Cocoa Frosting. Pierce warm cake with fork. Pour Cocoa Frosting over all. Cool completely. Cut in squares. Makes 16 servings.

Cocoa Frosting: Combine ½ c. butter or regular margarine, 6 tblsp. milk and ¼ c. baking cocoa in saucepan. Cook over medium heat until butter is melted and mixture is smooth. Stir in 1 (1 lb.) box confectioners sugar, sifted. Continue cooking over low heat until confectioners sugar is completely dissolved. Remove from heat. Stir in 1 tsp. vanilla. Frost cake immediately.

MAYONNAISE CHOCOLATE CAKE

"This is the only chocolate cake recipe my husband wants me to make—an heirloom from his mother. And according to my husband all chocolate cakes must have chocolate frosting—or they're not worth eating," wrote a Minnesota farm wife.

3 c. sifted flour	1½ c. sugar
⅓ c. baking cocoa	1½ c. cold water
3 tsp. baking soda	1½ tsp. vanilla
½ tsp. salt	Fluffy Chocolate Frosting
1½ c. mayonnaise or salad dressing	(recipe follows)

Sift together flour, cocoa, baking soda and salt; set aside.

Combine mayonnaise and sugar in mixing bowl. Beat with electric mixer at medium speed until blended. Gradually beat in cold water and vanilla.

Add dry ingredients to mayonnaise mixture, beating until well blended, about 2 minutes. Pour batter into greased 13x9x2" baking pan.

Bake in 350° oven 40 minutes or until cake tests done. Cool in pan on rack. Frost with Fluffy Chocolate Frosting. Cut in squares. Makes 16 servings.

Fluffy Chocolate Frosting: Combine 1 c. packed brown sugar, 3 tblsp. light cream and 3 tblsp. butter or regular margarine in saucepan. Cook over medium heat, stirring constantly, until mixture comes to a boil. Boil 1 minute. Remove from heat. Stir in ⅓ c. semisweet chocolate pieces and ½ tsp. vanilla. Beat with electric mixer at high speed until of spreading consistency.

BLACK MAGIC CAKE

"I used to throw leftover coffee and sour milk away until I discovered this recipe. Now I substitute sour milk for the buttermilk. Not only does it use two leftovers, but it is a cinch to make, as all ingredients are mixed in one bowl," wrote an Ohio farm wife. This is a super dark chocolate cake with a lighter chocolate frosting that's extra crunchy with nuts.

1¾ c. sifted flour
2 c. sugar
¾ c. baking cocoa
2 tsp. baking soda
1 tsp. baking powder
1 tsp. salt
2 eggs

½ c. cooking oil
1 c. strong black coffee
1 c. buttermilk
1 tsp. vanilla
Hundred Dollar Frosting
    (recipe follows)

Sift together flour, sugar, cocoa, baking soda, baking powder and salt into mixing bowl. Add eggs, oil, coffee, buttermilk and vanilla. Beat with electric mixer at medium speed 2 minutes. Pour batter into greased 13x9x2" baking pan.

Bake in 350° oven 40 minutes or until cake tests done. Cool in pan on rack. Frost with Hundred Dollar Frosting. Cut in squares. Makes 16 servings.

Hundred Dollar Frosting: Combine ¼ c. butter or regular margarine and 3 (1 oz.) squares semisweet chocolate in double boiler top. Place over hot water, stirring until melted. Remove and cool well. Add 1 egg; stir vigorously. Stir in 2 c. sifted confectioners sugar, 1 tblsp. vanilla and 1 tblsp. lemon juice. Beat until smooth. Stir in 1 c. chopped walnuts.

ZUCCHINI/CHOCOLATE CAKE

"Every summer we have an overabundance of zucchini in our garden. This quick and easy cake recipe helps use up the surplus," wrote a South Dakota woman. *"My family would be happy if I made this cake every day."*

2½ c. sifted flour
¼ c. baking cocoa
1 tsp. baking soda
1 tsp. salt
½ c. butter or regular
   margarine
½ c. cooking oil
1¾ c. sugar

2 eggs
1 tsp. vanilla
½ c. buttermilk
2 c. grated unpared
   zucchini
1 (6 oz.) pkg. semisweet
   chocolate pieces
¾ c. chopped walnuts

Sift together flour, cocoa, baking soda and salt; set aside.

Cream together butter, oil and sugar in mixing bowl until light and fluffy, using electric mixer at medium speed. Beat in eggs, one at a time, beating well after each addition. Blend in vanilla.

Add dry ingredients alternately with buttermilk to creamed mixture, beating well after each addition. Stir in zucchini. Pour batter into greased 13x9x2" baking pan. Sprinkle with chocolate pieces and walnuts.

Bake in 325° oven 55 minutes or until cake tests done. Cool in pan on rack. Cut in squares. Makes 16 servings.

RED BEET CHOCOLATE CAKE

"This is our very special cake," wrote a Missouri woman. "It's a deep chocolate color with a mild flavor." She started to make this cake when her garden was overflowing with beets and the family was tired of eating buttered beets every night for dinner. Now the more beets in the garden, the happier the family is as they know they can count on Mom's "good beet" cake for dessert.

1¾ c. sifted flour
1½ tsp. baking soda
½ tsp. salt
1½ c. sugar
3 eggs
1 c. cooking oil
1½ c. pureed beets

2 (1 oz.) squares
   unsweetened chocolate,
   melted and cooled
1 tsp. vanilla
Sifted confectioners
   sugar

Sift together flour, baking soda and salt; set aside.

Combine sugar, eggs and oil in mixing bowl. Beat with electric mixer at medium speed 2 minutes. Beat in beets, cooled chocolate and vanilla.

Gradually add dry ingredients, beating well after each addition. Pour into greased 13x9x2" baking pan.

Bake in 350° oven 25 minutes or until cake tests done. Cool in pan on rack. Cover and let stand overnight to improve flavor. Sprinkle with confectioners sugar. Makes 16 servings.

CHOCOLATE SAUERKRAUT CAKE

"No one will ever guess that there is sauerkraut in this cake unless you tell them," wrote an Ohio farm wife. "The sauerkraut shreds almost disappear as the cake bakes and taste like crunchy coconut."

2¼ c. sifted flour
½ c. baking cocoa
1 tsp. baking powder
1 tsp. baking soda
¼ tsp. salt
⅔ c. butter or
   regular margarine
1½ c. sugar

3 eggs
1 tsp. vanilla
1 c. water
⅔ c. sauerkraut, rinsed,
   drained and chopped
Creamy Chocolate
   Frosting (recipe follows)

Sift together flour, cocoa, baking powder, baking soda and salt; set aside.

Cream together butter and sugar in bowl until light and fluffy, using electric mixer at medium speed. Add eggs, one at a time, beating well after each addition. Beat in vanilla.

Add dry ingredients alternately with water to creamed mixture, beating well after each addition. Stir in sauerkraut. Spread batter in greased 13x9x2" baking pan.

Bake in 350° oven 35 minutes or until cake tests done. Cool in pan on rack. Frost with Creamy Chocolate Frosting. Cut in squares. Makes 16 servings.

Creamy Chocolate Frosting: Melt 1 (1 oz.) square semisweet chocolate in custard cup in hot water. Cool slightly. Combine cooled chocolate, 1 (3 oz.) pkg. cream cheese, softened, 1 tblsp. milk, 1 c. sifted confectioners sugar, ⅛ tsp. salt and ½ tsp. vanilla in bowl. Beat with electric mixer at high speed until smooth and creamy.

WHIMSICAL CHOCOLATE BIRTHDAY CAKE

Standing three layers high, this magnificent cake has won four blue ribbons for an Indiana woman. Decorate with easy chocolate cutouts in animal or other shapes made with cookie cutters.

2¼ c. sifted flour	1¾ c. sugar
1 tsp. baking soda	3 eggs
¾ tsp. salt	1 tsp. vanilla
1 (6 oz.) pkg. semisweet	1 c. buttermilk
chocolate pieces	Chocolate Cutouts
¼ c. water	(recipe follows)
¾ c. butter or regular	Seafoam Frosting (recipe
margarine	follows)

Sift together flour, baking soda and salt; set aside.

Combine chocolate pieces and water in saucepan. Cook over low heat, stirring constantly, until chocolate melts. Cool to room temperature.

Cream together butter and sugar in mixing bowl until light and fluffy, using electric mixer at medium speed. Add eggs, one at a time, beating well after each addition. Beat in vanilla and cooled chocolate mixture.

Add dry ingredients alternately with buttermilk to creamed mixture, beating well after each addition. Pour batter into 3 greased and waxed paper-lined 9" round cake pans.

Bake in 375° oven 25 to 30 minutes or until cakes test done. Cool in pans on racks 10 minutes. Remove from pans; cool on racks.

Meanwhile, prepare Chocolate Cutouts.

Place one cake layer on serving plate. Spread with Seafoam Frosting. Top with second cake layer; spread with frosting. Top

28

with third cake layer. Frost sides and top of cake with remaining Seafoam Frosting. Decorate top and sides of cake with Chocolate Cutouts. Makes 12 servings.

Chocolate Cutouts: Melt 4 (1 oz.) squares semisweet chocolate in double boiler top over hot water. Spread melted chocolate ⅛" thick on waxed paper-lined baking sheet. Refrigerate until firm. Cut into animal or other desired shapes, using cookie cutters. Carefully remove shapes from waxed paper. Refrigerate until needed.

Seafoam Frosting: Combine 2 c. packed brown sugar, ¾ c. water and 1 tblsp. light corn syrup in 2-qt. saucepan. Cover and bring to a boil over medium heat. Remove cover and cook to 236° on candy thermometer. Meanwhile, beat 2 egg whites in mixing bowl until stiff peaks form, using electric mixer at high speed. Pour hot syrup in thin stream into egg whites and beat constantly until mixture is thick and fluffy.

SOUR CREAM/CHOCOLATE LAYER CAKE

"This is everyone's birthday cake choice at our house," wrote a good cook from Missouri. "It's the moistest cake I've ever made—keeps beautifully. The recipe appeared years ago on the back of a flour bag—I revised it to suit my taste."

2 c. sifted flour	2 eggs
2 c. sugar	1 c. water
1¼ tsp. baking soda	4 (1 oz.) squares
½ tsp. baking powder	unsweetened chocolate,
1 tsp. salt	melted and cooled
¼ c. shortening	Sour Cream/Chocolate
¾ c. dairy sour cream	Frosting (recipe follows)
1 tsp. vanilla	

Sift together flour, sugar, baking soda, baking powder and salt into large mixing bowl. Add shortening, sour cream, vanilla, eggs, water and cooled chocolate. Beat with electric mixer at low speed ½ minute, scraping bowl constantly. Beat 3 more minutes at high speed, scraping bowl occasionally. Pour batter into 2 greased and waxed paper-lined 9" round cake pans.

Bake in 350° oven 35 minutes or until cakes test done. Cool in pans on racks 10 minutes. Remove from pans; cool on racks.

Place one cake layer on serving plate. Spread with Sour Cream/Chocolate Frosting. Top with second cake layer. Frost sides and top of cake with remaining Sour Cream/Chocolate Frosting. Makes 12 servings.

Sour Cream/Chocolate Frosting: Combine ⅓ c. soft butter or regular margarine, 3 c. sifted confectioners sugar and ½ c. dairy sour cream in mixing bowl; blend well. Add 3 (1 oz.) squares unsweetened chocolate, melted and cooled, and 1 tsp. vanilla. Beat until smooth.

GRANDMA'S CHOCOLATE LAYER CAKE

"The cake and frosting belong together. I never make one without the other," a Michigan woman told us. "Everyone raves about this whenever I make it—every crumb disappears—never any left over."

2¼ c. sifted flour
1 tsp. baking powder
½ tsp. baking soda
½ tsp. salt
¾ c. butter or regular
    margarine
1½ c. sugar
2 eggs

1 tsp. vanilla
2 (1 oz.) squares
    unsweetened chocolate,
    melted and cooled
1 c. cold water
Dark Chocolate Icing
    (recipe follows)

Sift together flour, baking powder, baking soda and salt; set aside.

Cream together butter and sugar in mixing bowl until light and fluffy, using electric mixer at medium speed. Add eggs, one at a time, beating well after each addition. Blend in vanilla and cooled chocolate.

Add dry ingredients alternately with water to creamed mixture, beating well after each addition. Pour batter into 2 greased and waxed paper-lined 9" round cake pans.

Bake in 350° oven 30 minutes or until cakes test done. Cool in pans on racks 10 minutes. Remove from pans; cool on racks.

Place one cake layer on serving plate. Spread with Dark Chocolate Icing. Top with second cake layer. Frost sides and top of cake with remaining Dark Chocolate Icing. Makes 12 servings.

Dark Chocolate Icing: Melt 3 (1 oz.) squares unsweetened chocolate over hot water. Cool to room temperature. Combine ½ c. soft butter or regular margarine, cooled chocolate and 3 egg yolks in mixing bowl. Beat with electric mixer until well blended. Gradually beat in 1 (1 lb.) box sifted confectioners sugar and ¼ c. hot water. Beat in 1 tsp. vanilla.

CHOCOLATE CHIFFON LAYER CAKE

"So good—so tender—so economical—so easy to make . . . what else can I say? It's our favorite chocolate cake," wrote a Kansas farm woman. We agree; it's superb!

1¾ c. sifted cake flour	2 (1 oz.) squares
1 c. sugar	unsweetened chocolate,
¾ tsp. baking soda	melted and cooled
¾ tsp. salt	½ c. sugar
⅓ c. cooking oil	Vanilla Cream Frosting
1 c. buttermilk	(recipe follows)
2 eggs, separated	1 c. flaked coconut

Sift together cake flour, 1 c. sugar, baking soda and salt into large mixing bowl. Add oil and one half of buttermilk. Beat 1 minute, using electric mixer at medium speed, scraping bowl constantly. Add remaining buttermilk, egg yolks and cooled chocolate. Beat 1 more minute.

Beat egg whites in another bowl until frothy. Gradually add ½ c. sugar, beating until stiff glossy peaks form, using electric mixer at high speed. Fold egg white mixture into chocolate mixture. Pour batter into 2 greased and waxed paper-lined 9" round cake pans.

Bake in 350° oven 25 to 30 minutes or until cakes test done. Cool in pans on racks 10 minutes. Remove from pans; cool on racks.

Place one cake layer on serving plate. Spread with Vanilla Cream Frosting. Top with second cake layer. Frost sides and top of cake with remaining Vanilla Cream Frosting. Sprinkle with coconut. Makes 12 servings.

Vanilla Cream Frosting: Sift 1 (1 lb.) box confectioners sugar into mixing bowl. Add ½ c. soft butter or regular margarine, 1½ tsp. vanilla and 4 tblsp. milk. Beat until smooth.

OLD WORLD CHOCOLATE CAKE

"A recipe that's been in our family for several generations. We think it might be originally from Germany," said an Indiana homemaker. "Buttermilk makes the cake velvety and tender and the flavor of coffee filters through."

1½ c. sifted cake flour	⅔ c. shortening
1¼ c. sugar	1 c. buttermilk
⅓ c. baking cocoa	1 tsp. vanilla
1 tblsp. instant coffee	2 eggs
powder	Sweetened Whipped Cream
1¼ tsp. baking soda	(recipe follows)
¾ tsp. salt	

Sift together cake flour, sugar, cocoa, coffee powder, baking soda and salt into large mixing bowl. Add shortening, ⅔ c. of the buttermilk and vanilla. Beat with electric mixer at medium speed 2 minutes. Add remaining ⅓ c. buttermilk and eggs. Beat 2 more minutes. Pour batter into 2 greased 8" round cake pans.

Bake in 350° oven 30 minutes or until cakes test done. Cool in pans on racks 10 minutes. Remove from pans; cool on racks.

Place one cake layer on serving plate. Spread with Sweetened

Whipped Cream. Top with second cake layer. Frost cake with Sweetened Whipped Cream. Refrigerate until serving time. Makes 12 servings.

Sweetened Whipped Cream: Chill mixing bowl and beaters. Place 1 c. heavy cream, 2 tblsp. sugar and 1 tsp. vanilla in chilled bowl. Beat with electric mixer at high speed until soft peaks form and mixture is of spreading consistency. Do not overbeat.

EGYPTIAN CHOCOLATE CAKE

"My husband discovered this recipe during World War II when he was in the service," a North Dakota woman wrote us. This is for chocolate fans who like a strong chocolate flavor. The spices and coffee make it different. And the Cinnamon Whipped Cream frosting makes it extra special.

1¾ c. sifted flour	1 c. sugar
2 tsp. baking powder	2 eggs
1 tsp. ground cinnamon	1 tsp. vanilla
⅛ tsp. ground cloves	½ c. milk
4 (1 oz.) squares semisweet chocolate	Cinnamon Whipped Cream (recipe follows)
½ c. strong coffee	
½ c. butter or regular margarine	

Sift together flour, baking powder, cinnamon and cloves; set aside.

Combine chocolate and coffee in small saucepan. Cook over low heat until chocolate is melted, stirring constantly. Remove from heat and cool to room temperature.

Cream together butter and sugar in mixing bowl until light and

34

fluffy, using electric mixer at medium speed. Add eggs, one at a time, beating well after each addition. Beat in vanilla and chocolate mixture.

Add dry ingredients alternately with milk to creamed mixture, beating well after each addition. Pour batter in 2 greased and waxed paper-lined 8" round cake pans.

Bake in 350° oven 30 minutes or until cakes test done. Cool in pans on racks 10 minutes. Remove from pans; cool on racks.

Place one cake layer on serving plate. Spread with Cinnamon Whipped Cream. Top with second cake layer. Frost sides and top of cake with remaining Cinnamon Whipped Cream. Refrigerate until serving time. Makes 12 servings.

Cinnamon Whipped Cream: Chill large mixing bowl and beaters. Combine 2 c. heavy cream, ¼ c. sugar, 2 tsp. vanilla and ½ tsp. ground cinnamon in chilled bowl. Beat with electric mixer at high speed until soft peaks form and mixture is thick enough to spread. Do not overbeat.

MILE-HIGH CHOCOLATE CAKE

Very high, very elegant three-layer beauty, filled and frosted with a creamy Cocoa Icing. "When I entered this cake 26 years ago at our County Fair I won a blue ribbon. My daughter won another 'blue' four years ago when she entered it. Need I say this is definitely my family's favorite chocolate cake?" a Texas woman wrote us.

½ c. baking cocoa	2 tsp. vanilla
½ c. hot water	2½ c. sifted flour
2 tsp. baking soda	1 c. buttermilk
½ c. shortening	Cocoa Icing (recipe
2 c. sugar	follows)
2 eggs	

35

Combine cocoa, hot water and baking soda in small bowl. Let stand while mixing other ingredients.

Cream together shortening and sugar in mixing bowl until light and fluffy, using electric mixer at medium speed. Add eggs, one at a time, beating well after each addition. Beat in vanilla and cocoa mixture.

Add flour alternately with buttermilk to creamed mixture, beating well after each addition. Pour batter into 3 greased and waxed paper-lined 8" round cake pans.

Bake in 350° oven 25 minutes or until cakes test done. Cool in pans on racks 10 minutes. Remove from pans; cool on racks.

Place one cake layer on serving plate. Spread with Cocoa Icing. Top with second cake layer. Spread with icing. Top with third cake layer. Frost sides and top of cake with remaining Cocoa Icing. Makes 16 servings.

Cocoa Icing: Combine ½ c. butter or regular margarine and 1 (1 oz.) square unsweetened chocolate in double boiler top. Place over hot water; stir until melted. Remove from heat; cool to room temperature. Sift 1 (1 lb.) box confectioners sugar into large mixing bowl. Make a well in the center and add 1 egg white, 1 tsp. vanilla and 1 tsp. lemon juice. Pour in chocolate mixture. Blend until smooth, using electric mixer at medium speed. Add 3 tblsp. milk to make frosting of spreading consistency.

CHOCOLATE/LEMON LAYER CAKE

"Birthdays are very special at our house," a Wisconsin farm home-maker said. "A very special birthday cake is a must—this is our choice for all birthdays. We don't serve ice cream with this cake—you don't need it with the rich cocoa whipped filling."

2¼ c. sifted cake flour
1 tsp. baking soda
1 tsp. salt
¾ c. shortening
1½ c. sugar
4 eggs
1 tblsp. grated lemon rind
1 c. milk
3 (1 oz.) squares
   unsweetened chocolate,
   melted and cooled

Cocoa/Butter Filling
   (recipe follows)
2 c. heavy cream
¼ c. sugar
1 tsp. vanilla
20 pecan halves
½ (1 oz.) square
   semisweet chocolate,
   melted and cooled

Sift together cake flour, baking soda and salt; set aside.

Cream together shortening and 1½ c. sugar in mixing bowl until light and fluffy, using electric mixer at medium speed. Add eggs, one at a time, beating well after each addition. Beat in lemon rind.

Add dry ingredients alternately with milk to creamed mixture, beating well after each addition. Beat in cooled unsweetened chocolate. Pour batter into 2 greased and waxed paper-lined 9" round cake pans.

Bake in 350° oven 35 minutes or until cakes test done. Cool in pans on racks 10 minutes. Remove from pans; cool on racks.

Place one cake layer on serving plate. Spread with Cocoa/Butter Filling. Top with second cake layer.

Beat heavy cream in mixing bowl until it begins to thicken, using electric mixer at high speed. Gradually beat in ¼ c. sugar and vanilla. Beat until soft peaks form and mixture is of spreading consistency. Do not overbeat. Spread on sides and top of cake. Dip one end of each pecan half in cooled semisweet chocolate. Decorate top of cake with chocolate-dipped pecans. Refrigerate until serving time. Makes 12 servings.

Cocoa/Butter Filling: Cream together 1 c. soft butter or regular margarine and ¾ c. sifted confectioners sugar in mixing bowl until light and fluffy. Beat in ½ c. baking cocoa and 1 tsp. vanilla; blend until smooth.

BASIC CHOCOLATE LAYER CAKE

"This is the only cake my family wants me to make," wrote a West Virginia farm woman. "The batter is very thin—don't add extra flour," she warned. "I've been baking this cake for 25 years and still haven't found one I like as well."

2 c. sifted cake flour	2 (1 oz.) squares
1½ tsp. cream of	unsweetened chocolate,
tartar	melted and cooled
½ tsp. salt	½ c. milk
½ c. butter or regular	1 tsp. baking soda
margarine	¾ c. boiling water
1¼ c. sugar	Chocolate 7-Minute
2 eggs	Frosting (recipe follows)
1 tsp. vanilla	

Sift together cake flour, cream of tartar and salt; set aside.

Cream together butter and sugar in mixing bowl until light and fluffy, using electric mixer at medium speed. Beat in eggs, one at a time, beating well after each addition. Blend in vanilla and cooled chocolate.

Add dry ingredients alternately with milk to creamed mixture, beating well after each addition. Dissolve baking soda in boiling water and quickly blend into chocolate mixture. (Batter is very thin.) Pour into 2 greased and waxed paper-lined 9" round cake pans.

Bake in 350° oven 25 minutes or until cakes test done. Cool in pans on racks 10 minutes. Remove from pans; cool on racks.

Place one cake layer on serving plate. Spread with Chocolate 7-Minute Frosting. Top with second cake layer. Frost sides and top of cake with remaining Chocolate 7-Minute Frosting. Makes 12 servings.

Chocolate 7-Minute Frosting: Combine 2 egg whites, 1½ c. sugar, ⅓ c. water and ¼ tsp. cream of tartar in top of double boiler. Beat with electric mixer at high speed for 1 minute. Place over simmering water. Cook 7 minutes, beating constantly at high speed, until soft glossy peaks form. Remove from hot water. Beat in 1 tsp. vanilla. Fold in 2 (1 oz.) squares unsweetened chocolate, melted and cooled.

DELUXE CHOCOLATE LAYER CAKE

A heavenly fine-textured cake that a Michigan farm wife has made for years. (See photo, Plate 5.) In Farm Journal's Test Kitchens, we developed a coffee frosting that makes this cake superlative.

2½ c. sifted cake flour	4 eggs
1½ tsp. baking soda	2¼ c. sugar
¾ tsp. salt	1½ tsp. vanilla
3 (1 oz.) squares	1½ c. dairy sour cream
unsweetened chocolate	Chocolate Cutouts
¾ c. milk	(recipe follows)
5 tsp. butter or	Mocha Fluff Frosting
regular margarine	(recipe follows)

Sift together cake flour, baking soda and salt; set aside.

Combine chocolate, milk and butter in saucepan. Cook over low heat, stirring constantly, until mixture thickens (about 10 minutes). Remove from heat; cool to room temperature.

Beat eggs in mixing bowl until thickened, using electric mixer at high speed. Gradually add sugar, beating until mixture is very thick and lemon-colored. Beat in vanilla.

Add dry ingredients alternately with sour cream to egg mixture, beating well after each addition. Blend in chocolate mixture, beating at medium speed 2 minutes. Pour batter into 3 greased and waxed paper-lined 8" round cake pans.

Bake in 350° oven 35 minutes or until cakes test done. Cool in pans on racks 10 minutes. Remove from pans; cool on racks.

Meanwhile, prepare Chocolate Cutouts.

Place one cake layer on serving plate. Spread with Mocha Fluff Frosting. Top with second cake layer; spread with frosting. Top with third cake layer. Frost sides and top of cake with remaining

Mocha Fluff Frosting. Decorate top of cake with Chocolate Cutouts. Refrigerate cake until serving time. Makes 12 servings.

Chocolate Cutouts: Melt 2 (1 oz.) squares semisweet chocolate in custard cup in hot water. Spread melted chocolate ⅛" thick on waxed paper-lined baking sheet. Refrigerate until firm. Cut into shapes using small cookie or aspic cutters. Carefully remove shapes from waxed paper. Refrigerate until needed.

Mocha Fluff Frosting: Combine 2 c. heavy cream and 1 tblsp. instant coffee powder in large mixing bowl. Refrigerate 20 minutes. Combine 1 (7½ oz.) jar marshmallow creme, 1 tblsp. hot water and 1 tsp. vanilla in another bowl. Beat with electric mixer at high speed until smooth and creamy, about 3 minutes. Whip chilled coffee mixture with electric mixer at high speed until soft peaks form. Gradually fold marshmallow mixture into whipped cream mixture.

CREAM CHEESE/CHOCOLATE CAKE

Our test kitchen home economist shared her mother's extra-special cake with us. A unique cake—the chocolate cream cheese frosting is made first and part of it is used in the batter of the cake.

2 c. sifted cake flour	¼ c. hot water
1½ tsp. baking soda	4 (1 oz.) squares
1 tsp. salt	unsweetened chocolate,
2 (3 oz.) pkgs. cream cheese	melted and cooled
½ c. shortening	¼ c. shortening
2 tsp. vanilla	3 eggs
6 c. sifted confectioners	¾ c. milk
sugar	1 tblsp. milk

Sift together cake flour, baking soda and salt; set aside.

Combine cream cheese, ½ c. shortening and vanilla in large mixing bowl. Beat with electric mixer at high speed until light and fluffy. Add confectioners sugar alternately with hot water and cooled chocolate to cream cheese mixture, beating well after each addition. Blend until smooth. Remove 2 c. chocolate mixture and cover with plastic wrap. Reserve for frosting.

Blend ¼ c. shortening into remaining chocolate mixture. Add eggs, one at a time, beating well after each addition. Add dry ingredients alternately with ¾ c. milk, beating well after each addition. Spread batter in 2 greased and waxed paper-lined 9" round cake pans.

Bake in 350° oven 35 minutes or until cakes test done. Cool in pans on racks 10 minutes. Remove from pans; cool on racks.

Blend 1 tblsp. milk into 2 c. reserved chocolate mixture for frosting. Place one cake layer on serving plate. Spread with frosting. Top with second cake layer. Frost sides and top of cake with remaining frosting. Makes 12 servings.

PRIZE-WINNING CHOCOLATE CAKE

Four scrumptious chocolate layers filled and frosted with rich chocolate cheese filling—looks like an elegant torte. A California woman shared this recipe with us—it's her most requested cake at family gatherings and a blue ribbon winner, too!

---

3 (1 oz.) squares
   semisweet chocolate
½ c. water
Red food color
2½ c. sifted cake flour
1 tsp. baking soda
½ tsp. salt
1 c. butter or regular
   margarine

2 c. sugar
4 eggs, separated
1 tsp. vanilla
1 c. buttermilk
Chocolate/Cheese Filling
   (recipe follows)

Combine chocolate and water in small saucepan. Cook over low heat until chocolate is melted. Stir in a few drops red food color. Remove from heat. Cool to room temperature.

Sift together cake flour, baking soda and salt; set aside.

Cream together butter and sugar in mixing bowl until light and fluffy, using electric mixer at medium heat. Add egg yolks, one at a time, beating well after each addition. Blend in vanilla and cooled chocolate mixture.

Add dry ingredients alternately with buttermilk to creamed mixture, beating well after each addition.

Beat egg whites in another bowl until stiff peaks form, using electric mixer at high speed. Fold egg whites into chocolate mixture. Pour batter into 4 greased and waxed paper-lined 9" round cake pans.

Bake in 350° oven 35 minutes or until cakes test done. Cool in pans on racks 10 minutes. Remove from pans; cool on racks.

Place one cake layer on serving plate. Spread Chocolate/ Cheese Filling between layers and on top of cake. Refrigerate overnight for best results. Makes 12 servings.

Chocolate/Cheese Filling: Cream together ¼ c. soft butter or regular margarine and 1 (8 oz.) pkg. cream cheese in mixing bowl, using electric mixer at medium speed. Beat in 3 (1 oz.) squares semisweet chocolate, melted and cooled, dash of salt, a few drops of red food color and 1 tsp. vanilla. Add 4 c. sifted confectioners sugar alternately with ⅓ c. light cream, beating well after each addition.

DELIGHTFUL APRICOT/FUDGE CAKE

"A great cake," a Texas woman wrote us when she submitted this recipe. And it's nutritious, too, chock-full of tangy dried apricots. All chocolate fans who prefer the deep dark chocolate flavor will love this cake. The sweetened whipped cream filling and frosting is the perfect choice for this tender-crumbed beauty.

⅔ c. chopped dried apricots	2 eggs
1 c. water	3 (1 oz.) squares
2 c. sifted flour	unsweetened chocolate,
2½ tsp. baking powder	melted and cooled
¼ tsp. baking soda	1 tsp. vanilla
½ tsp. salt	¾ c. milk
½ c. butter or regular	Sweetened Cream Filling
margarine	(recipe follows)
1¼ c. sugar	

Combine apricots and water in 1-quart saucepan. Bring to a boil. Boil gently, uncovered, 3 minutes. Remove from heat. Cool well. Drain off liquid.

Sift together flour, baking powder, baking soda and salt; set aside.

Cream together butter and sugar in mixing bowl until light and fluffy, using electric mixer at medium speed. Add eggs, one at a time, beating well after each addition. Blend in cooled chocolate and vanilla.

Add dry ingredients alternately with milk, ,beating well after each addition. Blend in apricots. Pour batter into 2 greased and waxed paper-lined 8" round cake pans.

Bake in 350° oven 35 minutes or until cakes test done. Cool in pans on racks 10 minutes. Remove from pans; cool on racks.

Place one cake layer on serving plate. Spread with one half of Sweetened Cream Filling. Top with second cake layer. Spread top of cake with remaining Sweetened Cream Filling. Refrigerate until serving time. Makes 10 servings.

Sweetened Cream Filling: Chill mixing bowl and beaters. Combine 1 c. heavy cream, 2 tblsp. sugar and 1 tsp. vanilla in chilled bowl. Beat with electric mixer at high speed until soft peaks form and mixture is of spreading consistency. Do not overbeat.

CHOCOLATE-LEMON CAKE

Three thin layers of rich, firm-textured fudge cake filled and topped with a tangy chocolate-lemon frosting. The shaved chocolate garnish adds a final elegant touch. (See photo, Plate 3.) Looks like a cake you'd find in an expensive French bakery.

2 c. sifted flour	4 (1 oz.) squares
2 tsp. baking powder	unsweetened chocolate,
1 tsp. salt	melted and cooled
½ c. butter or	2 tsp. vanilla
regular margarine	1¼ c. milk
2 c. sugar	Chocolate-Lemon Frosting
4 eggs	(recipe follows)

Sift together flour, baking powder and salt; set aside.

Cream together butter and sugar in bowl until light and fluffy, using electric mixer at medium speed. Add eggs, one at a time, beating well after each addition. Blend in cooled chocolate and vanilla.

Add dry ingredients alternately with milk to creamed mixture, beating well after each addition. Pour batter into 3 greased and waxed paper-lined 9" round cake pans.

Bake in 350° oven 30 minutes or until cakes test done. Cool in pans on racks 10 minutes. Remove from pans; cool on racks.

Place one cake layer on serving plate. Spread with one third of Chocolate-Lemon Frosting. Top with second layer. Spread with one third of frosting. Top with third layer. Spread with remaining Chocolate-Lemon Frosting. Decorate with shaved chocolate, if you wish. Makes 16 servings.

Chocolate-Lemon Frosting: Combine ½ c. soft butter or regular margarine, 1 c. sifted confectioners sugar, 3 (1 oz.) squares semi-sweet chocolate, melted and cooled, and 1 egg in bowl. Beat with electric mixer at high speed until smooth and creamy. Add 3 c. sifted confectioners sugar, 1 tsp. vanilla, ¼ tsp. salt and 1 tblsp. grated lemon rind. Beat until frosting is smooth. Add a little milk, if necessary, to make frosting of spreading consistency.

CHOCOLATE VELVET CAKE

"I'm submitting a chocolate cake recipe that has been in our family for years," wrote a South Dakota farm woman (See photo, Plate 6). "A birthday party wasn't complete if we didn't have Chocolate Velvet Cake all aglow with candles," she said. Now her children are grown, but they still expect to have "Mom's chocolate cake" at special family occasions.

3 (1 oz.) squares
    unsweetened chocolate
1 c. water
½ c. butter or
    regular margarine
2 c. sugar
3 eggs
2½ c. sifted cake flour
1½ tsp. baking soda

1 c. buttermilk
1 tsp. vanilla
Creamy Coffee Frosting
    (recipe follows)
1 (1 oz.) square
    unsweetened chocolate
1 tsp. butter or
    regular margarine

Combine 3 squares chocolate and water in saucepan. Heat until it comes to a boil. Cool well.

Cream together ½ c. butter and sugar in bowl until light and fluffy, using electric mixer at medium speed for 2 minutes. Add eggs, one at a time, beating well after each addition.

Sift together cake flour and baking soda. Add flour mixture alternately with buttermilk to creamed mixture, beating well after each addition. Blend in chocolate mixture and vanilla. Pour into 2 greased and waxed paper-lined 9" round cake pans.

Bake in 350° oven 35 minutes or until cakes test done. Cool in pans on racks 10 minutes. Remove from pans; cool on racks.

Place one cake layer on serving plate. Spread with Creamy Coffee Frosting. Top with second cake layer. Frost sides and top of cake with remaining Creamy Coffee Frosting.

Then melt 1 square chocolate and 1 tsp. butter in saucepan over low heat; stir occasionally. Cool slightly. Spoon chocolate along edge of cake, allowing it to drip down sides. Makes 12 servings.

Creamy Coffee Frosting: Combine 2 tsp. instant coffee crystals and 2 tblsp. hot water; set aside. Combine ¾ c. soft butter or regular margarine, 6 c. sifted confectioners sugar, 1 tsp. vanilla, 4 tblsp. milk and coffee mixture in large bowl. Beat with electric mixer at medium speed until smooth and creamy.

SPEEDY CHOCOLATE SHEET CAKE

A rich chocolate cake that a California woman makes often, as she can tote the cake right in the pan to a potluck supper.

2 c. sifted flour	1 c. water
2 c. sugar	½ c. buttermilk
1 tsp. baking soda	2 eggs
½ tsp. salt	1 tsp. vanilla
1 c. butter or regular	Pecan/Chocolate Glaze
margarine	(recipe follows)
3 tblsp. baking cocoa	

Sift together flour, sugar, baking soda and salt into mixing bowl.

Combine butter, cocoa and water in saucepan. Cook over medium heat, stirring constantly, until mixture comes to a boil. Remove from heat. Add to dry ingredients with buttermilk, eggs and vanilla. Beat with electric mixer at medium speed until smooth. (Batter is thin.) Pour into greased 15½x10½x1" jelly roll pan.

Bake in 350° oven 30 minutes or until cake tests done. Cool in pan on rack 15 minutes. Meanwhile, prepare Pecan/Chocolate Glaze. Pour glaze over warm cake. Cool completely and cut in squares. Makes 24 servings.

Pecan/Chocolate Glaze: Combine ½ c. butter or regular margarine, 5 tblsp. baking cocoa and ⅓ c. milk in saucepan. Cook over medium heat until butter melts. Remove from heat. Sift 1 (1 lb.) box confectioners sugar into mixing bowl. Pour in hot chocolate mixture and 1 c. chopped pecans. Mix with spoon until smooth.

BUTTERMILK BROWNIE SHEET CAKE

A Wisconsin farm wife feels that if a recipe is made with buttermilk, it always turns out beautifully, especially if it's a chocolate cake. This is her cake to take to family reunions—even the frosting is rich in buttermilk!

2 c. sifted flour	½ c. cooking oil
2 c. sugar	2 eggs
¼ c. baking cocoa	1 tsp. baking soda
1 c. water	½ c. buttermilk
¼ c. butter or regular margarine	Buttermilk Frosting (recipe follows)

Sift together flour, sugar and cocoa into mixing bowl.

Combine water, butter and oil in saucepan. Cook over medium heat just until butter melts. Add butter mixture to dry ingredients. Beat with electric mixer at medium speed 1 minute.

Add eggs; beat 2 more minutes. Dissolve baking soda in buttermilk; blend into chocolate mixture. Pour batter into greased 15½x10½x1" jelly roll pan.

Bake in 350° oven 25 minutes or until cake tests done. Cool in pan on rack 15 minutes. Meanwhile, prepare Buttermilk Frosting. Spread on warm cake. Cool completely and cut in squares. Makes 24 servings.

Buttermilk Frosting: Combine ⅓ c. butter or regular margarine, 2 tblsp. buttermilk and 2 tblsp. baking cocoa in saucepan. Cook, stirring constantly, until butter is melted. Place 2 c. sifted confectioners sugar in mixing bowl. Stir in hot cocoa mixture. Beat with electric mixer at medium speed until smooth and creamy.

CHOCOLATE SHEET CAKE WITH COCOA/NUT FROSTING

"My Mother sent me this recipe," said a Colorado ranch woman. "I always take this cake to wedding showers and graduation parties." She always tucks the recipe into her purse because she knows she will have at least a dozen requests for it.

2 c. sifted flour	1 tsp. baking soda
2 c. sugar	½ c. buttermilk
½ c. butter or regular margarine	2 eggs
½ c. shortening	1 tsp. vanilla
¼ c. baking cocoa	Cocoa/Nut Frosting
1 c. water	(recipe follows)

Sift together flour and sugar into mixing bowl.

Combine butter, shortening, cocoa and water in saucepan. Cook over medium heat until butter and shortening are melted. Pour into flour mixture. Beat with electric mixer at medium speed until blended. Dissolve baking soda in buttermilk. Add to chocolate mixture with eggs and vanilla. Beat until smooth. Pour batter into greased 15½x10½x1" jelly roll pan.

Bake in 400° oven 20 minutes or until cake tests done. Cool in pan on rack. Meanwhile, prepare Cocoa/Nut Frosting. Spread over warm cake. Cool completely and cut in squares. Makes 24 servings.

Cocoa/Nut Frosting: Combine ½ c. butter or regular margarine, 3 tblsp. baking cocoa and ⅓ c. milk in saucepan. Cook over medium heat just until butter melts. Remove from heat. Add 2 c. sifted confectioners sugar, 1 tsp. vanilla and 1 c. chopped walnuts. Beat with spoon until smooth.

50

MARASCHINO CHERRY/
CHOCOLATE CAKE

A very, very mild flavored chocolate cake with bright red maraschino cherries folded into the batter. A pretty cake to serve at Christmastime as it is decorated with cherries and looks so festive.

1½ c. sifted flour
1 tsp. baking soda
¼ tsp. salt
½ c. butter or regular
   margarine
1 c. sugar
1 egg
1 (1 oz.) square
   unsweetened chocolate,
   melted and cooled

1 c. buttermilk
¼ c. chopped maraschino
   cherries, well drained
Confectioners Sugar Icing
   (recipe follows)
Halved maraschino cherries

Sift together flour, baking soda and salt. Reserve 1 tblsp. flour mixture; set aside.

Cream together butter and sugar in bowl until light and fluffy, using electric mixer at medium speed. Beat in egg and chocolate.

Add dry ingredients alternately with buttermilk to creamed mixture, beating well after each addition. Mix chopped cherries with reserved 1 tblsp. flour mixture. Add to batter; mix well. (Batter will look curdled.) Spread in greased 9" square baking pan.

Bake in 350° oven 40 minutes or until cake tests done. Cool in pan on rack. Frost with Confectioners Sugar Icing. Decorate with halved cherries. Cut in squares. Makes 9 servings.

Confectioners Sugar Icing: Combine 2 c. sifted confectioners sugar, 3 tblsp. soft butter or regular margarine, pinch of salt and

½ tsp. vanilla in bowl. Beat with electric mixer at medium speed until smooth and creamy, adding 1 more tblsp. milk if necessary.

CHOCOLATE/VINEGAR CAKE

A Minnesota woman discovered this recipe in a very old church cookbook and was intrigued with the way the cake was put together. Her kids love to watch her make it and call it "Mom's real dark chocolate cake."

1½ c. sifted flour	1 tblsp. vinegar
1 c. sugar	5 tblsp. butter or regular
3 tblsp. baking cocoa	margarine, melted
1 tsp. baking soda	1 c. water
½ tsp. salt	Mocha/Chocolate Frosting
1 tsp. vanilla	(recipe follows)

Sift together flour, sugar, cocoa, baking soda and salt into mixing bowl. Make 3 wells in dry ingredients. Pour vanilla into 1 well; vinegar into 1 well and butter into the third. Pour water over all. Beat with spoon until well blended. Pour batter into greased 9" square baking pan.

Bake in 350° oven 25 minutes or until cake tests done. Cool in pan on rack. Frost with Mocha/Chocolate Frosting. Cut in squares. Makes 9 servings.

Mocha/Chocolate Frosting: Combine 1¾ c. sifted confectioners sugar, 3 tblsp. baking cocoa, 3 tblsp. soft butter or regular margarine, 3 tblsp. hot coffee and ½ tsp. vanilla in bowl. Beat with electric mixer at medium speed until smooth.

MOIST CHOCOLATE LOAF

*According to a Farm Journal reader from Texas, this cake origi-
nated in a famous hotel in New York City and the going price for
the recipe was $100. She received it free from a friend.*

2½ c. sifted flour	2 tsp. vanilla
2 tsp. baking powder	4 (1 oz.) squares
½ tsp. salt	unsweetened chocolate,
½ c. butter or regular	melted and cooled
margarine	1½ c. milk
2 c. sugar	2 c. chopped walnuts
3 eggs	Sifted confectioners sugar

Sift together flour, baking powder and salt; set aside.

Cream together butter and sugar in bowl until light and fluffy,
using electric mixer at medium speed. Add eggs, one at a time,
beating well after each addition. Beat in vanilla and chocolate.

Add dry ingredients alternately with milk to creamed mixture,
beating well after each addition. Stir in walnuts. Spread batter
into 2 greased 9x5x3" loaf pans.

Bake in 350° oven 50 minutes or until cakes test done. Cool in
pans on racks 10 minutes. Remove from pans; cool on racks. Dust
with confectioners sugar before serving. Cut in slices, 10 in each
loaf. Makes 20 servings.

PUMPKIN/CHOCOLATE CAKE

"Our favorite fall and winter cake," wrote an Illinois woman."I have never tasted a cake like it, with all the different ingredients. And the amount of spice is just right." We thought so, too, and plan on baking this unusual pumpkin cake for Thanksgiving.

2 c. sifted flour	4 eggs
2 c. sugar	1 (1 lb.) can pumpkin
2 tsp. baking powder	1 c. cooking oil
1 tsp. baking soda	1 c. whole bran cereal
½ tsp. salt	1 (6 oz.) pkg. semisweet
1½ tsp. ground cinnamon	chocolate pieces
½ tsp. ground cloves	1 c. chopped walnuts
¼ tsp. ground ginger	Confectioners Sugar Glaze
¼ c. ground allspice	(recipe follows)

Sift together flour, sugar, baking powder, baking soda, salt, cinnamon, cloves, ginger and allspice; set aside.

Beat eggs in large mixing bowl until foamy, using electric mixer at high speed. Add pumpkin, oil and cereal; beat thoroughly. Add dry ingredients all at once, stirring just until blended. Stir in chocolate pieces and walnuts. Spread in well-greased 10" tube pan.

Bake in 350° oven 1 hour or until wooden pick inserted near center comes out clean. Cool in pan on rack. Remove from pan. Drizzle with Confectioners Sugar Glaze. Makes 12 servings.

Confectioners Sugar Glaze: Combine 1½ c. sifted confectioners sugar, 2 tblsp. water and ¼ tsp. vanilla in bowl. Blend until smooth and creamy.

CHOCOLATE CREAM CAKE

A New York farm woman acquired this recipe at a church "recipe swap." "My husband likes it because it is a good solid cake—not spongy as air, like so many of those fancy cakes," she wrote.

3 c. sifted flour	**3 eggs**
½ c. baking cocoa	**1 tsp. vanilla**
2 tsp. baking soda	**1 c. milk**
2 tsp. baking powder	**1 c. boiling water**
½ tsp. salt	**Sifted confectioners**
¾ c. shortening	**sugar**
2 c. sugar	

Sift together flour, cocoa, baking soda, baking powder and salt; set aside.

Cream together shortening and sugar in mixing bowl until light and fluffy, using electric mixer at medium speed. Add eggs, one at a time, beating well after each addition. Blend in vanilla.

Add dry ingredients alternately with milk to creamed mixture, beating well after each addition. Blend in boiling water. Pour batter into well-greased 10" tube pan.

Bake in 325° oven 1 hour or until cake tests done. Cool in pan on rack 10 minutes. Remove from pan; cool on rack. Dust with confectioners sugar. Makes 12 servings.

MAGIC CHOCOLATE SWIRL CAKE

A marbled beauty! We understand why a North Carolina homemaker receives lots of compliments whenever she takes this cake to reunions, picnics and club meetings. Serve plain or with the glaze.

2¾ c. sifted flour
1 tsp. baking soda
½ tsp. salt
1 c. butter or regular
   margarine
2 c. sugar
3 eggs

2 tsp. vanilla
1 c. buttermilk
1 c. chocolate-flavored
   syrup
¼ tsp. baking soda
Satiny Chocolate Glaze
   (recipe follows)

Sift together flour, baking soda and salt; set aside.

Cream together butter and sugar in bowl until light and fluffy, using electric mixer at medium speed. Add eggs, one at a time, beating well after each addition. Blend in vanilla.

Add dry ingredients alternately with buttermilk to creamed mixture, beating well after each addition. Reserve 2 c. batter. Pour remaining batter into well-greased 10" fluted tube pan. Combine chocolate-flavored syrup and baking soda; mix well. Mix syrup mixture into 2 c. reserved batter, blending well. Pour chocolate batter over vanilla batter in pan. Do not mix.

Bake in 350° oven 1 hour or until cake tests done. Cool in pan on rack 15 minutes. Remove from pan; cool on rack. Drizzle cake with Satiny Chocolate Glaze. Makes 12 servings.

Satiny Chocolate Glaze: Combine ½ c. semisweet chocolate pieces, 3 tblsp. butter or regular margarine, 1 tblsp. light corn syrup and ¼ tsp. vanilla in small saucepan. Cook over low heat, stirring constantly, until chocolate is melted and mixture is smooth.

MOCHA CHIFFON CAKE

A super light cake with a moist, velvety crumb. The mocha glaze is much thicker than most, so it forms big fat "drips" that slide down the side of the cake. Looks yummy and old-fashioned.

1¾ c. sifted cake flour	¾ c. boiling water
1¾ c. sugar	½ c. cooking oil
1½ tsp. baking soda	7 eggs, separated
1 tsp. salt	2 tsp. vanilla
2 tsp. instant coffee powder	½ tsp. cream of tartar
½ c. baking cocoa	Coffee Glaze (recipe follows)

Sift together cake flour, sugar, baking soda and salt into large mixing bowl. Make a well in the center.

Combine coffee powder, cocoa and boiling water in another bowl. Mix to blend. Add to well in dry ingredients along with oil, egg yolks and vanilla. Beat with electric mixer at medium speed for 3 minutes.

Beat egg whites with cream of tartar in large mixing bowl until stiff peaks form, using electric mixer at high speed. Fold egg whites into batter. Pour into ungreased 10" tube pan. Cut through batter with metal spatula to break up large air bubbles.

Bake in 325° oven 65 minutes or until cake tests done. Invert cake and cool completely. Remove from pan. Drizzle with Coffee Glaze. Makes 12 servings.

Coffee Glaze: Combine 2 tblsp. plus 2 tsp. milk, 1½ tsp. instant coffee powder and 2 tblsp. butter or regular margarine in small saucepan. Cook over low heat until butter melts. Sift 2 c. sifted confectioners sugar into bowl. Add coffee mixture and ½ tsp. vanilla. Blend with spoon until smooth and creamy.

MEXICAN CHOCOLATE CAKE

"My two daughters always choose this for their birthday cake," a Wisconsin woman told us. "They like the cake frosted with the white icing, but when I serve it to guests, I just dust the top with confectioners sugar or serve plain topped with ice cream."

⅓ c. baking cocoa	½ c. cooking oil
¾ c. hot coffee	8 eggs, separated
1¾ c. sifted flour	1 tsp. vanilla
1⅔ c. sugar	½ tsp. cream of tartar
1½ tsp. baking soda	Fluffy Frosting
½ tsp. salt	(recipe follows)

Combine cocoa and coffee in bowl. Blend until cocoa is dissolved. Set aside to cool.

Sift together flour, sugar, baking soda and salt into large mixing bowl. Make a well in the center. Add cooled coffee mixture, oil, egg yolks and vanilla. Beat with electric mixer at medium speed for 3 minutes.

Beat egg whites with cream of tartar until stiff peaks form, using electric mixer at high speed. Fold egg whites into batter. Pour batter into ungreased 10" tube pan. Cut through batter with metal spatula to break large air bubbles.

58

Bake in 325° oven 50 minutes. Increase oven temperature to 350° and bake 15 more minutes or until cake tests done. Invert cake to cool.

Remove cake from pan. Place on serving plate. Frost with Fluffy Frosting. Makes 12 servings.

Fluffy Frosting: Combine 1 c. sugar, ⅓ c. water, ¼ tsp. cream of tarter and ¹/₁₆ tsp. salt in small saucepan. Cook over medium heat, stirring constantly, until mixture comes to a boil. Continue boiling until candy thermometer reads 242° and mixture spins a 6" thread. Meanwhile, beat 2 egg whites until soft peaks form, using electric mixer at high speed. Gradually add hot syrup in a thin stream to egg whites, beating constantly at high speed. Continue beating until frosting is very fluffy and of spreading consistency. Beat in ½ tsp. vanilla.

CHOCOLATE PECAN SPONGE CAKE

This cake has all the qualities of a light and airy sponge cake, plus it's chocolate too! Surprise your favorite man on his birthday— make this handsome cake and serve with chocolate ice cream.

---

1 (6 oz.) pkg. semisweet chocolate pieces	1 tsp. salt
	6 eggs
1¼ c. water	1 tsp. vanilla
2 tsp. instant coffee powder	1½ c. sugar
	½ c. finely chopped pecans
1¾ c. sifted flour	Confectioners Sugar Glaze
1½ tsp. baking soda	(recipe follows)

Combine chocolate pieces, water and coffee powder in top of double boiler. Place over hot water and heat until chocolate melts. Remove from heat. Cool to room temperature.

Sift together flour, baking soda and salt; set aside.

Beat eggs and vanilla in large mixing bowl until foamy, using electric mixer at high speed. Gradually add sugar, beating until very thick and lemon colored, about 5 minutes.

Add dry ingredients alternately with cooled chocolate mixture, beating well after each addition. Stir in pecans. Pour batter into well greased 10" fluted tube pan or tube pan.

Bake in 350° oven 1 hour or until cake tests done. Cool in pan on rack 10 minutes. Remove from pan; cool on rack. Drizzle with Confectioners Sugar Glaze. Makes 12 servings.

Confectioners Sugar Glaze: Combine 1 c. sifted confectioners sugar, 4 tsp. water and ½ tsp. vanilla in bowl. Beat with spoon until smooth.

CHOCOLATE ANGEL FOOD CAKE

"My husband has never liked angel food cake—but when I made this chocolate angel, he ate three pieces," a Pennsylvania farm wife told us. Now he always asks when I'm going to make the fluffy chocolate cake. My children expect it on birthdays."

1½ c. sifted confectioners sugar	1½ c. egg whites (about 12 large eggs)
¾ c. sifted cake flour	1½ tsp. cream of tartar
¼ c. baking cocoa	¼ tsp. salt
1 tsp. instant coffee powder	1 c. sugar

Sift together confectioners sugar, cake flour, cocoa and coffee powder two times. Set aside.

Combine egg whites, cream of tartar and salt in large mixing bowl. Beat with electric mixer at high speed until foamy. Gradually add sugar, 2 tblsp. at a time, beating until stiff peaks form.

Fold dry ingredients into egg white mixture in four additions. Spread batter in ungreased 10" tube pan. Cut through batter with metal spatula to break large air bubbles.

Bake in 375° oven 35 minutes or until cracks on top of cake look dry and surface springs back when lightly touched. Invert cake to cool. Remove from pan. Makes 12 servings.

SOUTHERN POUND CAKE

A golden crusted cake that needs no frosting (See photo, Plate 3.) Delicious, rich and moist—with a swirl of chocolate in the center.

So good served with a scoop of vanilla ice cream for a special company dessert.

2½ c. sifted flour	2½ c. sugar
1¼ tsp. baking powder	5 eggs
½ tsp. salt	1 c. less 2 tblsp. milk
1¼ c. soft butter	2 tsp. vanilla
or regular margarine	¼ c. baking cocoa

Sift together flour, baking powder and salt; set aside.

Cream together butter and sugar in bowl until light and fluffy, using electric mixer at medium speed. Add eggs, one at a time, beating well after each addition.

Add dry ingredients alternately with milk to creamed mixture, beating well after each addition. Blend in vanilla.

Remove 2 c. cake batter; place in small bowl. Stir in cocoa. Alternately spoon vanilla and chocolate batter into greased and floured 10" tube pan or 10" fluted tube pan. Pull metal spatula through batter creating a marbled effect.

Bake in 325° oven 70 minutes or until cake tests done. Cool in pan on rack 10 minutes. Remove from pan; cool on rack. Dust with confectioners sugar before serving, if you wish. Makes 12 servings.

ELEGANT CHOCOLATE LOG

A spectacular dessert to serve at teas, receptions and graduation parties. (See photo, Plate 7.) If you plan to make this for a crowd of twenty, make two logs, place them end to end on your prettiest tray and frost as one.

1¼ c. sifted
confectioners sugar
¼ c. plus 1 tblsp.
sifted flour
½ tsp. salt
5 tblsp. baking cocoa
6 eggs, separated
¼ tsp. cream of tartar
1¼ tsp. vanilla
1 tblsp. water

1 c. heavy cream
2 tblsp. sugar
12 marshmallows, cut up
1 (1 oz.) square
unsweetened chocolate,
melted and cooled
2 c. sifted confectioners
sugar
Light cream
¼ c. chopped pecans

Sift together 1¼ c. confectioners sugar, flour, salt and cocoa 3 times; set aside.

Beat egg whites with cream of tartar in bowl until stiff peaks form, using electric mixer at high speed. Set aside.

Beat egg yolks in another bowl until thick and lemon-colored, using electric mixer at high speed. Beat in vanilla and water. Blend in dry ingredients, beating well. Fold in beaten egg whites. Spread batter in greased and waxed paper-lined 15½x10½x1" jelly roll pan.

Bake in 375° oven 15 to 20 minutes or until cake tests done. Meanwhile, lightly dust a clean dish towel with confectioners sugar. Loosen cake around edges with spatula and invert cake on towel. Lift off pan and carefully peel off paper. With a sharp knife, cut off crisp edges. Roll up cake gently, from narrow end, by folding edge of cake over and then tucking it in towel. Continue rolling cake, using towel as aid. Let cake cool in towel on rack.

Whip heavy cream in bowl until thickened, using electric mixer at high speed. Add sugar, beating until soft peaks form. Fold in marshmallows. Unroll cake. Spread with cream mixture. Reroll.

Combine cooled chocolate and 2 c. confectioners sugar in bowl. Add enough light cream to make a frosting of spreading consistency. Spread over cake roll. Sprinkle with pecans. Refrigerate until serving time. Makes 10 servings.

CHOCOLATE CUPCAKES WITH CHOCOLATE GLAZE

A Nebraska woman wrote us that her aunt made these cupcakes for years. Although her aunt had no children of her own, she enjoyed surprising her nieces and nephews with cupcake treats when they came to visit. They loved to watch her swirl the cupcakes in the shiny glaze. (See photo, Plate 4.)

1 (18½ oz.) pkg. chocolate cake mix	4 eggs
1 (4 oz.) pkg. chocolate pudding and pie filling (not instant)	¾ c. cooking oil
	¾ c. water
	Chocolate Glaze (recipe follows)

Combine cake mix, pudding mix, eggs, oil and water in mixing bowl. Beat with electric mixer at medium speed 2 minutes. Spoon batter into paper-lined 2½" muffin-pan cups, filling one-half full.

Bake in 375° oven 15 minutes or until cupcakes test done. Remove from pans; cool on racks. Dip cupcake tops in Chocolate Glaze. Makes 36 cupcakes.

Chocolate Glaze: Combine 2 c. miniature marshmallows, ¾ c. sugar, ¹/₁₆ tsp. salt, ½ c. evaporated milk and ¼ c. butter or regular margarine in 2-qt. saucepan. Bring to a boil, stirring constantly. Boil 3 minutes, stirring constantly. Remove from heat. Stir in 1 (6 oz.) pkg. semisweet chocolate pieces. Stir until chocolate pieces are melted. Place saucepan in cold water. Beat with wooden spoon until frosting begins to thicken.

FUDGE CUPCAKES WITH MAPLE FROSTING

Maple and chocolate make a delicious team. "Sure would hate to misplace this recipe," wrote an Iowan. Brown sugar gives a different flavor to the cupcakes.

⅔ c. brown sugar, packed
⅓ c. milk
2 (1 oz.) squares
   unsweetened chocolate
1⅓ c. sifted flour
1 tsp. baking soda
½ tsp. salt
⅔ c. shortening

⅔ c. brown sugar, packed
2 eggs
1 tsp. vanilla
½ c. milk
Maple Frosting (recipe
   follows)
24 walnut halves

Combine ⅔ c. brown sugar, ⅓ c. milk and chocolate in small saucepan. Cook over low heat, stirring constantly, until chocolate is melted. Remove from heat; cool to room temperature.

Sift together flour, baking soda and salt; set aside.

Cream together shortening and ⅔ c. brown sugar in mixing bowl until light and fluffy, using electric mixer at medium speed. Add eggs, one at a time, beating well after each addition. Beat in vanilla.

Add dry ingredients alternately with ½ c. milk to creamed mixture, beating well after each addition. Beat in cooled chocolate mixture. Spoon batter into paper-lined 2½" muffin-pan cups, filling one-half full.

Bake in 375° oven 20 minutes or until cupcakes test done. Remove from pans; cool on racks. Frost with Maple Frosting and top each with walnut half. Makes 24 cupcakes.

Maple Frosting: Combine 2 c. sifted confectioners sugar, 3 tblsp. soft butter or regular margarine, 2 tblsp. milk, 1 tsp. maple flavoring and ½ tsp. vanilla in bowl. Beat with electric mixer at medium speed until smooth and creamy.

CHOCOLATE CUPCAKES WITH PEANUT BUTTER FROSTING

"Easy to make and always 'top sellers' at bake sales and church suppers," a Minnesota woman wrote.

3 c. sifted flour	2 c. water
2 c. sugar	2 tsp. vinegar
½ c. baking cocoa	2 tsp. vanilla
2 tsp. baking soda	Peanut Butter Frosting
1 tsp. salt	(recipe follows)
1 c. cooking oil	

Sift together flour, sugar, cocoa, baking soda and salt into mixing bowl. Make a well in the center of dry ingredients. Add oil, water, vinegar and vanilla. Beat with electric mixer at medium speed ½ minute or just until blended. Spoon batter into paper-lined 2½" muffin-pan cups, filling one-half full.

Bake in 350° oven 15 to 18 minutes or until cupcakes test done. Remove from pans; cool on racks. Frost with Peanut Butter Frosting. Makes 32 cupcakes.

Peanut Butter Frosting: Combine 2 c. sifted confectioners sugar, ¾ c. crunchy peanut butter, 2 tblsp. soft butter or regular margarine and 6 tblsp. milk in mixing bowl. Beat with electric mixer at medium speed until creamy.

CREME-FILLED CHOCOLATE CUPCAKES

Better plan on baking a double batch! Chocolate frosted cupcakes with a surprise filling. Chocolate fans of every age will love them!

2 c. sifted flour	**2 eggs**
1 tsp. baking soda	**1 c. cold water**
⅛ tsp. salt	**Vanilla Creme Filling**
½ c. shortening	**(recipe follows)**
1½ c. sugar	**Chocolate Icing**
2 (1 oz.) squares	**(recipe follows)**
unsweetened chocolate,	
melted and cooled	

Sift together flour, baking soda and salt; set aside.

Cream together shortening and sugar in bowl until light and fluffy, using electric mixer at medium speed. Add cooled chocolate, eggs, water and dry ingredients. Beat at medium speed 2 minutes. Spoon batter in paper-lined 2½" muffin-pan cups, filling two-thirds full.

Bake in 350° oven 20 minutes or until cupcakes test done. Remove from pans; cool on racks. Prepare Vanilla Creme Filling and place in cake decorating bag or tube with a large tip. Push tip into top of cupcake and force filling into each. Frost tops of cupcakes with Chocolate Icing. Makes 24 cupcakes.

Vanilla Creme Filling: Combine 1½ c. sifted confectioners sugar, ½ c. shortening, ¼ c. water and 2 tsp. vanilla in bowl. Beat with electric mixer at high speed 2 minutes or until light and fluffy.

Chocolate Icing: Combine 1½ c. sifted confectioners sugar, 1 egg yolk, 2 tblsp. soft butter or regular margarine, 1½ (1 oz.) squares unsweetened chocolate, melted and cooled, 3 tblsp. light cream and 1 tsp. vanilla in bowl. Beat with electric mixer at medium speed until smooth.

CHOCOLATE CUPCAKES WITH BROWNED BUTTER FROSTING

"My youngsters prefer a very mild chocolate, so this is their favorite cupcake," said a Kansas mother. We dressed up the cupcake with a browned butter frosting in our Farm Journal Test Kitchens.

1¼ c. sifted flour	¼ c. baking cocoa
½ tsp. baking powder	½ c. dairy sour cream
½ tsp. baking soda	1 egg
½ tsp. salt	½ tsp. vanilla
½ c. boiling water	Browned Butter Frosting
¼ c. shortening	(recipe follows)
1 c. sugar	

Sift together flour, baking powder, baking soda and salt; set dry ingredients aside.

Combine boiling water, shortening, sugar and cocoa in mixing bowl. Beat with electric mixer at medium speed until sugar is dissolved and shortening is almost melted.

Combine sour cream, egg and vanilla in another bowl; mix well. Add dry ingredients alternately with sour cream mixture to cocoa mixture, beating well after each addition. Spoon batter into paper-lined 2½" muffin-pan cups, filling one-half full.

Bake in 350° oven 22 minutes or until cupcakes test done. Remove from pans; cool on racks. Frost with Browned Butter Frosting. Makes 18 cupcakes.

Browned Butter Frosting: Melt ¼ c. butter in small saucepan over low heat. Continue heating until butter turns a delicate brown color. Combine 2¼ c. sifted confectioners sugar, browned butter, 2 tblsp. milk and ½ tsp. vanilla in bowl. Beat with electric mixer at medium speed until smooth and creamy.

COCONUT CREAM-FILLED CHOCOLATE CUPCAKES

Tastes just like a popular commercial chocolate coconut candy bar. Cupcakes have a macaroon topping and are dipped in a shiny glaze.

1 egg white	**1 tsp. salt**
¹/₁₆ tsp. salt	**⅔ c. shortening**
¼ c. sugar	**2 eggs**
1¾ c. flaked coconut	**1 tsp. vanilla**
2 tblsp. flour	**1 c. buttermilk**
2½ c. sifted flour	**½ c. water**
1½ c. sugar	**Shiny Chocolate Glaze**
½ c. baking cocoa	**(recipe follows)**
2 tsp. baking soda	

Beat egg white and ¹/₁₆ tsp. salt in bowl until frothy, using electric mixer at high speed. Gradually add ¼ c. sugar, beating until stiff glossy peaks form. Combine coconut and 2 tblsp. flour. Fold into egg white mixture; set aside.

Sift together 2½ c. flour, 1½ c. sugar, cocoa, baking soda and 1 tsp. salt into mixing bowl. Add shortening, eggs, vanilla, buttermilk and water. Beat with electric mixer at medium speed 3 minutes or until batter is smooth. Spoon batter into paper-lined 2½" muffin-pan cups, filling one-half full. Place 1 teaspoonful of coconut mixture in center of each. Lightly press down coconut mixture with spoon into batter.

Bake in 350° oven 20 minutes or until cupcakes test done. Remove from pan; cool on racks. Dip tops of cupcakes into Shiny Chocolate Glaze. Makes 34 cupcakes.

Shiny Chocolate Glaze: Combine 2 c. sugar, ½ c. milk and ½ c. shortening in 2-qt. saucepan. Bring mixture to a rolling boil, stirring constantly. Remove from heat; stir in 1 (6 oz.) pkg. semisweet chocolate pieces. Stir until chocolate is melted. Beat with wooden spoon until mixture begins to thicken, about 5 minutes.

TOLL HOUSE CUPCAKES

Absolutely scrumptious with a crunchy meringue-like topping. When we tested this recipe in our kitchens, every cupcake disappeared in less than 20 minutes.

1 c. plus 2 tblsp. sifted flour	6 tblsp. sugar
½ tsp. baking soda	6 tblsp. brown sugar, packed
⅛ tsp. salt	1 egg
½ c. butter or regular margarine	½ tsp. vanilla
	Chocolate/Nut Topping (recipe follows)

Sift together flour, baking soda and salt; set aside.

Cream together butter and sugars in bowl until light and fluffy, using electric mixer at medium speed. Add egg; beat 1 more minute. Blend in dry ingredients and vanilla. Place 1 rounded teaspoonful of dough in each paper-lined 2½" muffin-pan cup.

Bake in 375° oven 12 minutes. Meanwhile, prepare Chocolate/Nut Topping. Spoon on cupcakes. Continue baking 15 more minutes. Remove from pans; cool on racks. Makes 20 cupcakes.

Chocolate/Nut Topping: Combine ½ c. packed brown sugar, 1 egg and 1 tsp. vanilla in bowl. Beat with electric mixer at medium speed until thick. Stir in 1 (6 oz.) pkg. semisweet chocolate pieces and 1½ c. chopped walnuts.

MOCHA-FILLED CHOCOLATE CUPCAKES

A Minnesota homemaker explained why she calls these cupcakes her "never fails." "They never fail to turn out perfectly and I never fail to receive compliments on these cupcakes."

1½ c. sifted flour	½ c. sour milk*
1 c. sugar	½ c. hot water
½ c. baking cocoa	1 tsp. vanilla
1 tsp. baking soda	Mocha Fluff Frosting
½ tsp. salt	(recipe follows)
1 egg	Chocolate jimmies
½ c. shortening	

Sift together flour, sugar, cocoa, baking soda and salt into large bowl. Add egg, shortening, sour milk, hot water and vanilla. Beat with electric mixer at medium speed 2 minutes. Spoon batter into paper-lined 2½" muffin-pan cups, filling one-half full.

Bake in 350° oven 20 minutes or until cupcakes test done. Remove from pans; cool on racks. Prepare Mocha Fluff Frosting. Place one half of the frosting in a cake decorating bag or tube with a large tip. Push tip into top of each cupcake and force filling into each. Frost tops of cupcakes with remaining Mocha Fluff Frosting. Sprinkle with chocolate jimmies. Makes 22 cupcakes.

*To sour milk: Place 1½ tsp. vinegar in measuring cup. Add enough milk to make ½ c.

Mocha Fluff Frosting: Dissolve 1½ tsp. instant coffee powder in 5 tblsp. milk. Combine 6 tblsp. shortening, 3 c. sifted confectioners sugar, 1½ (1 oz.) squares unsweetened chocolate, melted and cooled, and coffee mixture in bowl. Beat with electric mixer at medium speed until light and fluffy.

PINEAPPLE/CHOCOLATE CUPCAKES

An Iowa woman has been making these cupcakes for her family for 18 years. Her youngsters love the pineapple-chocolate combination.

2 c. sifted flour	1 (8 ¼ oz.) can crushed
1 tsp. baking soda	pineapple
1 tsp. salt	⅓ c. water
½ c. shortening	1 (6 oz.) pkg. semisweet
½ c. sugar	chocolate pieces
2 eggs	Pineapple Frosting
½ tsp. vanilla	(recipe follows)

Sift together flour, baking soda and salt; set aside.

Cream together shortening and sugar in mixing bowl until light and fluffy, using electric mixer at medium speed. Add eggs, one at a time, beating well after each addition. Blend in vanilla.

Drain pineapple, reserving juice. Remove 3 tblsp. crushed pineapple; reserve for frosting.

Add dry ingredients alternately with reserved pineapple juice and water to creamed mixture, beating well after each addition. Stir in remaining pineapple and chocolate pieces. Spoon batter into paper-lined 2½" muffin-pan cups, filling one-half full.

Bake in 350° oven 20 minutes or until cupcakes test done. Remove from pans; cool on racks. Frost with Pineapple Frosting. Makes 18 cupcakes.

Pineapple Frosting: Combine 2½ c. sifted confectioners sugar, 3 tblsp. reserved crushed pineapple and 1 tsp. vanilla in bowl. Beat with spoon until smooth and creamy.

QUICK AND EASY CHOCOLATE CUPCAKES

A recipe that fits into a busy Minnesota farm woman's schedule. They're so speedy to make and the fact that there is no need for frosting is an added plus. They freeze beautifully.

1 (18½ oz.) pkg. chocolate cake mix
1 (8 oz.) pkg. cream cheese
⅓ c. sugar
1 egg
1 (6 oz.) pkg. semisweet chocolate pieces

Prepare chocolate cake mix according to package directions. Spoon batter into paper-lined 2½" muffin-pan cups, filling one-half full.

Combine cream cheese, sugar and egg in bowl. Beat with electric mixer at high speed 2 minutes or until smooth and creamy. Stir in chocolate pieces. Drop cream cheese mixture by teaspoonfuls into each muffin-pan cup.

Bake in 350° oven 20 minutes or until cupcakes test done. Remove from pans; cool on racks. Makes 30 cupcakes.

LIGHT CHOCOLATE BROWNIE CUPCAKES

"I am sending you a cupcake that we think is very different," wrote an Iowa farm wife. (See photo, Plate 6.) "They taste like a brownie and have pretty glazed crinkly tops. Men really like them—even better than cake!"

4 (1 oz.) squares	**1 tsp. vanilla**
semisweet chocolate	**1 c. sifted flour**
1 c. butter or	**1¾ c. sugar**
regular margarine	**4 eggs**
1 c. chopped walnuts	

Melt chocolate and butter in saucepan over low heat. Remove from heat. Add walnuts and vanilla.

Sift together flour and sugar into bowl. Add eggs; beat with electric mixer at medium speed until blended. Blend in chocolate mixture. Pour batter into paper-lined 2½" muffin-pan cups, filling one-half full.

Bake in 325° oven 35 minutes or until done. Makes 24.

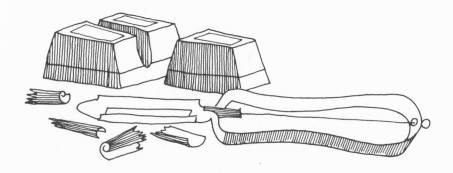

All kinds of Cookies

A farm mother once told us she always liked to keep the cookie jar full—it symbolized a warm and happy kitchen.

This chapter is full of recipes that can give your family and friends that same cookie-jar warmth and happiness.

There are Chocolate Mincemeat Jumbles for children to share with friends or plump Raisin Chocolate Cookies to munch while doing homework or watching T.V.

If you're planning to feed a hungry field crew, we suggest you make either the Whole Wheat/Raisin or the Cottage Cheese/Chocolate Cookies. Both of these rate first place with farm men, their wives told us when they sent in their recipes.

Bake a batch of bar cookies when you're in a hurry. Every recipe here is rich and full of chocolate. Consider trying the Butter Pecan Chocolate Bars, or Peanut Butter Fudge Bars or Chewy Chocolate Squares for starters. Teen-agers will love the wedge-shaped Chocolate Chip Pizza cookies baked in a pie plate.

Planning a wedding reception or fancy tea? Make the Chocolate Mint Creams and the Chocolate Refrigerator Cookies and arrange them on your prettiest tray—they look elegant indeed.

BROWNIE WALNUT DROPS

"I like to make this crackly topped cookie at Christmastime as it looks so pretty on a plate of assorted cookies. These always disappear first," wrote a Kansas woman. "They make nice gifts, too."

2 (4 oz.) pkgs. German sweet chocolate	¾ c. sugar
	¼ c. unsifted flour
1 tblsp. butter or regular margarine	¼ tsp. baking powder
	¼ tsp. ground cinnamon
2 eggs	⅛ tsp. salt
½ tsp. vanilla	¾ c. chopped walnuts

Combine German sweet chocolate and butter in small saucepan. Cook over low heat until melted. Remove from heat; cool to room temperature.

Beat eggs and vanilla in bowl until foamy, using electric mixer at high speed. Gradually add sugar, beating until thick and lemon-colored, about 5 minutes. Blend in cooled chocolate mixture.

Stir together flour, baking powder, cinnamon and salt. Add dry ingredients to chocolate mixture, mixing well. Stir in walnuts. Drop mixture by rounded teaspoonfuls, about 2" apart, on greased baking sheets.

Bake in 350° oven 10 minutes or until done. Cool slightly on baking sheets. Remove from baking sheets; cool on racks. Makes 2½ dozen.

CHOCOLATE/CHERRY DROPS

A fun variation of the basic chocolate chip cookie. A Texas woman received this recipe from a friend, then added and subtracted ingredi-

ents until it suited her family. Her grandchildren love the chewy maraschino cherries.

---

2 c. unsifted flour	**1 egg**
½ tsp. baking soda	**1 tblsp. vanilla**
½ tsp. salt	**1 (6 oz.) pkg. semisweet**
⅓ c. butter or regular	**chocolate pieces**
margarine	**½ c. chopped walnuts**
⅓ c. cooking oil	**½ c. chopped red maraschino**
½ c. sugar	**cherries, well drained**
½ c. brown sugar, packed	

Stir together flour, baking soda and salt; set aside.

Cream together butter, oil and sugars in bowl until light and fluffy, using electric mixer at medium speed. Add egg and vanilla, beating well.

Add dry ingredients to creamed mixture, mixing well. Stir in chocolate pieces, walnuts and cherries. Drop mixture by teaspoonfuls, about 2" apart, on ungreased baking sheets.

Bake in 375° oven 10 to 12 minutes or until golden brown. Remove from baking sheets; cool on racks. Makes 4 dozen.

BANANA FUDGE COOKIES

A flat drop cookie with a surprisingly strong flavor of banana that blends perfectly with the deep fudge flavor.

---

1 (18½ oz.) pkg.	**2 tblsp. water**
chocolate cake mix	**1 (6 oz.) pkg. semisweet**
⅓ c. mashed ripe bananas	**chocolate pieces**
1 egg	

Combine cake mix, bananas, egg and water in bowl. Beat with electric mixer at medium speed until smooth. Stir in chocolate pieces. Drop by rounded teaspoonfuls, about 2"apart, on greased baking sheets.

Bake in 350° oven 8 minutes or until done. Remove from baking sheets; cool on racks. Makes 3½ dozen.

FROSTED CHOCOLATE DROP COOKIES

A delightful variation of a basic chocolate cookie. A Nebraska woman revised her aunt's recipe and came up with this delicious raisin-filled cookie. She used her sister's glossy chocolate frosting.

1¾ c. unsifted flour	1 tsp. vanilla
½ c. baking cocoa	¾ c. buttermilk
½ tsp. baking soda	½ c. chopped raisins
½ tsp. salt	½ c. chopped walnuts
½ c. shortening	Chocolate Frosting
1 c. sugar	(recipe follows)
1 egg	

Stir together flour, cocoa, baking soda and salt; set aside.

Cream together shortening and sugar in bowl until light and fluffy, using electric mixer at medium speed. Add egg and vanilla, beating well.

Add dry ingredients alternately with buttermilk to creamed mixture, beating well after each addition. Stir in raisins and walnuts. Drop mixture by teaspoonfuls, about 2" apart, on ungreased baking sheets.

Bake in 350° oven 10 minutes or until done. Remove from baking sheets; cool on racks. Frost with Chocolate Frosting. Makes 4 dozen.

Chocolate Frosting: Combine 1 c. sugar, 1 (1 oz.) square unsweetened chocolate, ¼ c. butter or regular margarine and ⅓ c. milk in saucepan. Cook over medium heat, stirring constantly, until mixture boils. Boil 1½ minutes. Remove from heat. Place saucepan in bowl of cold water. Beat with electric mixer until frosting begins to hold its shape.

CHOCOLATE MARSHMALLOW COOKIES

"Don't be upset if the marshmallow topping is stringy when it first comes out of the oven," an Iowa woman warned us. "It mellows on standing. My family eats these as fast as I can bake them."

1¾ c. unsifted flour	1 tsp. vanilla
½ c. baking cocoa	½ c. milk
½ tsp. baking soda	½ c. chopped walnuts
½ tsp. salt	18 regular marshmallows, cut
½ c. shortening	in half
1 c. sugar	Cocoa Frosting
1 egg	(recipe follows)

Stir together flour, cocoa, baking soda and salt; set aside.

Cream together shortening and sugar in bowl until light and fluffy, using electric mixer at medium speed. Add egg and vanilla, beating well.

Add dry ingredients alternately with milk to creamed mixture, beating well after each addition. Stir in walnuts. Drop mixture by teaspoonfuls, about 2" apart, on ungreased baking sheets.

Bake in 350° oven 8 to 10 minutes. Top each with a marshmallow half, cut side down. Return to oven and bake 2 more minutes. Remove from baking sheets; cool on racks. Frost with Cocoa Frosting. Makes 3 dozen.

Cocoa Frosting: Sift together 2 c. sifted confectioners sugar, ⅓ c. baking cocoa and dash of salt into mixing bowl. Add 3 tblsp. melted butter or regular margarine, 4 tblsp. light cream and ½ tsp. vanilla. Mix until smooth and creamy.

CHOCOLATE SAUCEPAN COOKIES

"My husband's face really lights up when I tell him I have a batch of these cookies baking in the oven," an Iowa woman told us.

2 c. unsifted flour	**1½ tsp. vanilla**
½ tsp. baking powder	**2 (1 oz.) squares**
½ tsp. baking soda	**unsweetened chocolate,**
½ tsp. salt	**melted and cooled**
½ c. butter or	**½ c. milk**
regular margarine	**½ c. chopped walnuts**
1 c. brown sugar, packed	**Coffee/Chocolate Icing**
1 egg	**(recipe follows)**

Stir together flour, baking powder, baking soda and salt; set dry ingredients aside.

Melt butter in 2-qt. saucepan over low heat. Remove from heat. Stir in brown sugar; mix well. Add egg and vanilla; blend well. Blend in cooled chocolate.

Add dry ingredients alternately with milk to chocolate mixture, blending well after each addition. Stir in walnuts. Drop mixture by rounded teaspoonfuls, about 2" apart, on ungreased baking sheets.

Bake in 350° oven 8 minutes or until done. Remove from baking sheets; cool on racks. Frost with Coffee/Chocolate Icing. Makes 5 dozen.

Coffee/Chocolate Icing: Melt 1 (1 oz.) square unsweetened chocolate and 1 tblsp. butter or regular margarine in saucepan over low heat. Remove from heat. Add ½ tsp. instant coffee powder, 3 tblsp. hot water, ½ tsp. vanilla and 2 c. sifted confectioners sugar. Beat until smooth and creamy.

TRIPLE CHOCOLATE COOKIES

These feather-light cookies, made with sour cream and nuts and frosted with dark shiny chocolate frosting, have been all-time favorites for over 30 years in a New York family.

2 c. sifted flour	**2 eggs**
1 tsp. baking powder	**1 tsp. vanilla**
½ tsp. baking soda	**½ c. dairy sour cream**
¼ tsp. salt	**½ c. semisweet chocolate**
½ c. butter or	**pieces**
regular margarine	**½ c. chopped walnuts**
2½ (1 oz.) squares	**Chocolate Frosting**
unsweetened chocolate	**(recipe follows)**
1 c. sugar	

Sift together flour, baking powder, baking soda and salt; set dry ingredients aside.

Combine butter and chocolate in saucepan. Cook over low heat until melted. Remove from heat. Add sugar, eggs and vanilla. Beat with electric mixer until blended.

Add dry ingredients alternately with sour cream, mixing well. Stir in chocolate pieces and walnuts. Chill in refrigerator. Drop by teaspoonfuls, about 2" apart, on greased baking sheets.

Bake in 375° oven 10 to 12 minutes or until done. Remove from baking sheets; cool on racks. Frost with Chocolate Frosting. Makes 4 dozen.

Chocolate Frosting: Melt 2 (1 oz.) squares unsweetened chocolate and 2 tblsp. butter or regular margarine in saucepan over low heat. Remove from heat. Add 2 c. sifted confectioners sugar and 4 tblsp. milk. Beat until smooth and creamy.

CHOCOLATE SANDWICH COOKIES

"My boys request a batch of these cookies instead of a birthday cake," a Georgia woman said. Kids love the soft marshmallow filing and cake-like chocolate cookies.

2 c. sifted flour	**1 c. sugar**
½ c. baking cocoa	**1 egg**
1½ tsp. baking soda	**1 tsp. vanilla**
½ tsp. baking powder	**1 c. milk**
½ tsp. salt	**Marshmallow Filling**
½ c. butter or regular margarine	**(recipe follows)**

Sift together flour, cocoa, baking soda, baking powder and salt; set dry ingredients aside.

Cream together butter and sugar in bowl until light and fluffy, using electric mixer at medium speed. Add egg and vanilla; beat until well blended.

Add dry ingredients alternately with milk to creamed mixture, beating well after each addition. Drop mixture by rounded tablespoonfuls, about 3" apart, on greased baking sheets. Make an indentation in center of each with back of spoon. (This helps cookies to flatten during baking.)

Bake in 400° oven 7 minutes or until done. Remove from baking sheets; cool on racks. Spread one cookie with Marshmallow Filling. Top with another cookie to form a sandwich. Makes 2½ dozen sandwich cookies.

Marshmallow Filling: Cream together ½ c. shortening and 2 c. sifted confectioners sugar in bowl, using electric mixer at medium speed. Beat in 1 (7 oz.) jar marshmallow creme, 1 tsp. vanilla and 1 tblsp. milk. Beat until smooth and creamy.

NUTRITIOUS CHOCOLATE DROPS

A cookie that not only tastes good—it's good for you. Made with buttermilk baking mix and loaded with whole bran cereal and nuts. A Texas woman told us that her youngsters love to come home from school and smell these favorites baking in the oven.

2 (1 oz.) squares unsweetened chocolate	**1 egg**
¼ c. butter or regular margarine	**½ c. milk**
	1 tsp. vanilla
1½ c. buttermilk baking mix	**1 c. flaked coconut**
	1 c. whole bran cereal
¾ c. sugar	**1 c. chopped pecans**

Melt chocolate and butter in saucepan over low heat. Remove from heat; cool to room temperature.

Combine baking mix, sugar, egg, milk, vanilla and cooled chocolate mixture in bowl. Beat with electric mixer at medium speed until light and fluffy, about 2 minutes. Stir in coconut, bran cereal and pecans. Drop mixture by heaping teaspoonfuls, about 2" apart, on ungreased baking sheets.

Bake in 375° oven 8 minutes or until a slight imprint remains on surface of cookie when touched lightly with fingertip. Remove from baking sheets; cool on racks. Makes 4 dozen.

CHOCOLATE/WALNUT KISSES

A light airy meringue cookie filled with chocolate chips, corn flakes and coconut. "They are both 'chewy and crunchy,' " a South Dakota

*farm wife explained. "If I don't hide them, my family will devour an
entire batch while they are still cooling on the racks."*

3 egg whites	1 c. flaked coconut
½ tsp. cream of tartar	½ c. semisweet chocolate
1 c. sugar	pieces
½ tsp. vanilla	½ c. chopped walnuts
3 c. corn flakes	

Beat egg whites with cream of tartar in bowl until foamy, using
electric mixer at high speed. Gradually beat in sugar, beating until
stiff peaks form. Add vanilla.

Combine corn flakes, coconut, chocolate pieces and walnuts in
large bowl. Carefully fold in egg white mixture. Drop by heaping
teaspoonfuls, about 2" apart, on lightly greased baking sheets.

Bake in 350° oven 15 minutes or until meringues are lightly
browned. Immediately remove from baking sheets; cool on racks.
(If kisses become too hard to remove from baking sheets; return
to oven a few minutes to soften.) Makes 4 dozen.

CHOCOLATE MINCEMEAT JUMBLES

*A South Dakota woman always makes these cookies to include in a
gift box for shut-ins during the holidays. A round moist cookie with
just the right amount of mincemeat for spice and flavor.*

2½ c. unsifted flour	1 c. sugar
2 tsp. baking soda	3 eggs
1 tsp. salt	1 (6 oz.) pkg. semisweet
½ c. butter or regular	chocolate pieces
margarine	1 c. prepared mincemeat

Stir together flour, baking soda and salt; set aside.

Cream together butter and sugar in bowl until light and fluffy, using electric mixer at medium speed. Add eggs, one at a time, beating well after each addition.

Add dry ingredients to creamed mixture, mixing well. Stir in chocolate pieces and mincemeat. Drop mixture by tablespoonfuls, about 3" apart, on lightly greased baking sheets.

Bake in 375° oven 9 minutes or until lightly browned. Cool on baking sheets a few seconds. Remove from baking sheets; cool on racks. Makes about 4½ dozen.

COTTAGE CHEESE/ CHOCOLATE COOKIES

A soft cake-like chocolate cookie flecked with cottage cheese. A favorite with all the men in a Kansas farm family.

2½ c. unsifted flour	1¾ c. sugar
½ c. baking cocoa	1 c. small curd creamed
1 tsp. baking soda	cottage cheese
1 tsp. baking powder	2 eggs
½ tsp. salt	1 tsp. vanilla
1 c. butter or regular margarine	

Stir together flour, cocoa, baking soda, baking powder and salt; set dry ingredients aside.

Cream together butter and sugar in bowl until light and fluffy, using electric mixer at medium speed. Add cottage cheese, eggs and vanilla; blend well.

Add dry ingredients to creamed mixture, mixing well. Drop by teaspoonfuls, about 2" apart, on ungreased baking sheets.

Bake in 350° oven 10 minutes or until done. Remove from baking sheets; cool on racks. Makes 5 dozen.

DEVIL'S FOOD COOKIES

A soft mounded cookie that stays fresh for at least a week. A favorite lunchbox treat from a Nebraska kitchen.

2 c. sifted flour	2 (1 oz.) squares
½ tsp. baking soda	unsweetened chocolate,
¼ tsp. salt	melted and cooled
½ c. butter or	¾ c. dairy sour cream
regular margarine	½ c. chopped walnuts
1 c. brown sugar, packed	Chocolate Icing
1 egg	(recipe follows)
1 tsp. vanilla	

Sift together flour, baking soda and salt; set aside.

Cream together butter and brown sugar in bowl until light and fluffy, using electric mixer at medium speed. Add egg; beat well. Blend in vanilla and cooled chocolate.

Add dry ingredients alternately with sour cream to creamed mixture, beating well after each addition. Stir in walnuts. Drop mixture by heaping teaspoonfuls, about 2" apart, on greased baking sheets.

Bake in 350° oven 10 minutes or until done. Remove from baking sheets; cool on racks. Frost with Chocolate Icing. Makes 4½ dozen.

Chocolate Icing: Melt 2 (1 oz.) squares unsweetened chocolate and 2 tblsp. butter or regular margarine in saucepan over low heat. Remove from heat. Stir in 2 c. sifted confectioners sugar, 2 tblsp. water and 1 tsp. vanilla. Beat until smooth and creamy.

WHOLE WHEAT/RAISIN COOKIES

"My husband likes anything that is made with whole wheat, and if it is chocolate too, then it is a real favorite," wrote an Indiana farm wife. "These are big, he-man size cookies."

2½ c. sifted flour	4 eggs
2½ c. stirred whole	2 tsp. vanilla
wheat flour	2 tsp. baking soda
½ tsp. salt	2 tblsp. hot water
1 c. butter or regular	1 (12 oz.) pkg. semisweet
margarine	chocolate pieces
½ c. shortening	1 c. raisins
1½ c. brown sugar, packed	1 c. chopped walnuts
1½ c. sugar	Sugar

Stir together flour, whole wheat flour and salt; set aside.

Cream together butter, shortening, brown sugar and 1½ c. sugar in bowl until light and fluffy, using electric mixer at medium speed. Add eggs, one at a time, beating well after each addition. Blend in vanilla.

Dissolve baking soda in hot water. Add to creamed mixture with dry ingredients, mixing well. Stir in chocolate pieces, raisins and walnuts. Drop mixture by heaping tablespoonfuls or small ice cream scoop on greased baking sheets, about 3" apart. Press to make 2½" circle, using glass dipped in sugar.

Bake in 350° oven 12 minutes or until golden brown. Remove from baking sheets; cool on racks. Makes 4 dozen (3¾") cookies.

RAISIN/CHOCOLATE COOKIES

Light golden cookies with darker edges. They are buttery crisp with a very mild chocolate flavor. "This cookie is filled with all the ingredients that my children love," wrote a West Virginia woman.

2½ c. sifted flour	2 eggs
1 tsp. baking soda	2 tblsp. milk
¼ tsp. salt	2 tsp. vanilla
1 c. butter or regular	2 c. raisins
margarine	1 (6 oz.) pkg. semisweet
¾ c. sugar	chocolate pieces
¾ c. brown sugar, packed	1 c. chopped walnuts

Sift together flour, baking soda and salt into large mixing bowl. Add butter, sugar, brown sugar, eggs, milk and vanilla. Beat with electric mixer at low speed until blended. Then beat at medium speed until fluffy. Stir in raisins, chocolate pieces and walnuts. Drop mixture by heaping teaspoonfuls, about 2" apart, on greased baking sheets.

Bake in 375° oven 9 minutes or until done. Remove from baking sheets; cool on racks. Makes 4½ dozen.

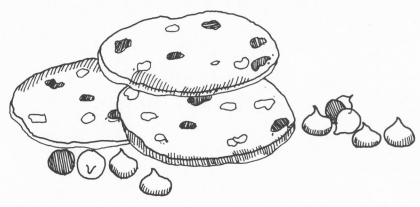

COCONUT/CHOCOLATE NUT DROPS

A large recipe that makes 6½ dozen chocolate cookies chock-full of nuts, coconut and chocolate pieces. Great for kids.

3 c. sifted flour	2 tsp. vanilla
1 tsp. baking soda	2 eggs
1 tsp. salt	1 tblsp. water
½ c. shortening	1 (12 oz.) pkg. semisweet
½ c. butter or regular	chocolate pieces
margarine	1 c. flaked coconut
1 c. sugar	1 c. chopped walnuts
1 c. brown sugar, packed	

Sift together flour, baking soda and salt; set aside.

Cream together shortening, butter and sugars in mixing bowl until light and fluffy, using electric mixer at medium speed. Add vanilla, eggs and water; beat well.

Stir dry ingredients into creamed mixture, mixing well. Stir in chocolate pieces, coconut and walnuts. Drop mixture by rounded teaspoonfuls, about 2" apart, on greased baking sheets.

Bake in 350° oven 12 minutes or until golden brown. Remove from baking sheets; cool on racks. Makes 6½ dozen.

CHOCOLATE LEBKUCHEN

"Many farmers have a German heritage," an Indiana woman told us. "And if you're German, you always have Lebkuchen at Christmastime. I would like to share my Chocolate Lebkuchen with you.

90

It's filled with spices, honey and half melted chocolate pieces. The longer it mellows, the better it tastes."

2¾ c. sifted flour	2 eggs
1 tsp. baking powder	¼ c. orange juice
1 tsp. baking soda	1 (12 oz.) pkg. semisweet
2 tsp. ground cinnamon	chocolate pieces
½ tsp. ground cloves	1 c. chopped walnuts
1½ tsp. ground cardamom	½ c. chopped mixed
1¼ c. sugar	candied fruit
¾ c. honey	Sifted confectioners sugar
2 tblsp. water	

Sift together flour, baking powder, baking soda, cinnamon, cloves and cardamom; set aside.

Combine sugar, honey and water in 2-qt. saucepan. Bring to a boil, stirring occasionally, over medium heat. Remove from heat. Pour into large mixing bowl. Cool to room temperature.

Add eggs and orange juice to cooled mixture. Beat 1 minute, using electric mixer at medium speed.

Add dry ingredients, beating 2 minutes at medium speed. Stir in chocolate pieces, walnuts and candied fruit. Spread batter in greased 15½x10½x1" jelly roll pan.

Bake in 325° oven 35 minutes or until done. Cool in pan on rack. Cover with aluminum foil. Store 3 days to develop flavor. Dust with confectioners sugar. Cut into 2" squares. Makes 35.

TOLL HOUSE BAR COOKIES

The famous Toll House Cookies baked into bars. Saves the fuss and bother of dropping dough by spoonfuls when you are in a hurry but want to fill the empty cookie jar before the youngsters come home from school.

2⅓ c. sifted flour	1 tsp. vanilla
1 tsp. baking soda	2 eggs
1 tsp. salt	1 (12 oz.) pkg. semisweet
1 c. soft butter or	chocolate pieces
regular margarine	1 c. chopped walnuts
¾ c. sugar	
¾ c. brown sugar, packed	

Sift together flour, baking soda and salt; set aside.

Cream together butter, sugar and brown sugar in bowl until light and fluffy, using electric mixer at medium speed. Beat in vanilla. Add eggs, one at a time, beating well after each addition.

Add dry ingredients, mixing well after each addition. Stir in chocolate pieces and walnuts. Spread mixture in greased 15½x10½x1" jelly roll pan.

Bake in 375° oven 20 minutes or until done. Cool in pan on rack. Cut into 2" squares. Makes 35.

BUTTER PECAN CHOCOLATE BARS

We agree with the Nebraska farm woman who sent us this cookie—it's rich, different and delicious.

2 c. sifted flour	⅔ c. butter or
1 c. brown sugar, packed	regular margarine
½ c. butter or	½ c. brown sugar, packed
regular margarine	1 (6 oz.) pkg. milk chocolate
1 c. pecan halves	pieces

Combine flour and 1 c. brown sugar in bowl. Cut in ½ c. butter until crumbly, using pastry blender. Press mixture into ungreased 13x9x2" baking pan. Sprinkle pecan halves over crust.

Combine ⅔ c. butter and ½ c. brown sugar in small saucepan. Cook over medium heat, stirring constantly, until mixture boils. Boil 1 minute. Pour over pecan halves.

Bake in 350° oven 20 minutes or until bubbly and crust is light brown. Remove from oven. Sprinkle chocolate pieces over all. Melt slightly and swirl chocolate through caramel layer for marbled effect. Cool in pan on rack. Cut into 3x1" bars. Makes 36.

CHOCOLATE CHIP PIZZA

"Our teenagers devour this in an evening," wrote a Washington woman. Wedge-shaped cookies filled with nuts, marshmallows and chocolate.

1 c. sifted flour	**1 egg**
½ tsp. baking powder	**1 tblsp. hot water**
⅛ tsp. baking soda	**1 tsp. vanilla**
½ tsp. salt	**½ c. chopped walnuts**
⅓ c. butter or regular margarine, melted	**1 (6 oz.) pkg. semisweet chocolate pieces**
1 c. brown sugar, packed	**1 c. miniature marshmallows**

Sift together flour, baking powder, baking soda and salt; set dry ingredients aside.

Combine melted butter and brown sugar in mixing bowl. Beat with electric mixer at medium speed until blended. Add egg, hot water and vanilla; mix well.

Add dry ingredients one third at a time, mixing well after each

93

addition. Stir in walnuts. Spread dough in 2 greased 9" pie plates. Sprinkle each with one half of chocolate pieces and one half of marshmallows.

Bake in 350° oven 20 minutes or until done. Cool in pans on racks. Cut each pie into 8 wedges. Makes 16 servings.

PEANUT BUTTER FUDGE BARS

An Iowa woman bakes batches of these rich, golden bars for bake sales and church bazaars. For a change, she switches to a chocolate cake mix instead of the yellow mix—makes it extra chocolatey.

1 (18½ oz.) pkg. yellow
  cake mix
1 c. creamy peanut butter
½ c. butter or
  regular margarine, melted
2 eggs
1 (15 oz.) can sweetened
  condensed milk

2 tblsp. butter or regular
  margarine, melted
2 tsp. vanilla
½ tsp. salt
1 (12 oz.) pkg. semisweet
  chocolate pieces
1 c. flaked coconut
1 c. chopped walnuts

Combine cake mix, peanut butter, ½ c. melted butter and eggs in bowl. Stir until well mixed. Press two thirds of mixture in bottom of ungreased 13x9x2" baking pan. Reserve remaining dough for topping.

Combine sweetened condensed milk (not evaporated), 2 tblsp. melted butter, vanilla and salt in bowl; mix well. Stir in chocolate pieces, coconut and walnuts. Spread over first layer. Crumble reserved dough evenly over filling.

Bake in 350° oven 25 to 30 minutes or until golden brown. Cool in pan on rack. Cut into 2x1" bars. Makes 48.

CHEWY CHOCOLATE SQUARES

A quick cookie made with chocolate pudding and pie filling mix and evaporated milk. Youngsters from a North Dakota family love the crunchy tops. Perfect for packed lunches.

---

1 c. unsifted flour	1 (3⅝ oz.) pkg. chocolate
¼ c. sifted confec-	pudding and pie filling
tioners sugar	½ tsp. baking powder
½ c. butter or	⅔ c. evaporated milk
regular margarine	1⅔ c. flaked coconut
¼ c. sugar	½ c. chopped pecans
1 egg	½ c. raisins

Combine flour and confectioners sugar in bowl. Cut in butter with pastry blender until crumbs form. Mix with hands, until mixture holds together. Press mixture into ungreased 8" square baking pan.

Bake in 350° oven 10 minutes. Place on rack. Prepare filling.

Combine sugar and egg in another bowl; beat until fluffy. Stir in pudding mix, baking powder and evaporated milk. Add coconut, pecans and raisins; mix well. Pour over baked crust.

Bake in 350° oven 30 minutes or until golden brown. Cool in pan on rack. Cut into 2" squares. Makes 16.

CHOCOLATE MINT CREAMS

A beautiful cookie to serve at showers or wedding receptions. Delicate cookies are filled with a creamy mint frosting, then one half is dipped in a chocolate glaze and decorated with tiny rosebuds made with a decorating tube. (See photo, Plate 4.)

2½ c. sifted flour	1 tsp. vanilla
1 tsp. baking soda	2 (1 oz.) squares
1 tsp. cream of tartar	unsweetened chocolate,
⅛ tsp. salt	melted and cooled
1 c. butter or regular	Mint Cream Filling
margarine	(recipe follows)
1½ c. sifted confectioners	Shiny Chocolate Glaze
sugar	(recipe follows)
1 egg	

Sift together flour, baking soda, cream of tartar and salt; set dry ingredients aside.

Cream together butter and confectioners sugar in bowl until light and fluffy, using electric mixer at medium speed. Add egg, vanilla and cooled chocolate, mixing well. Stir in dry ingredients, mixing well. Shape dough into 2 rolls, about 10" long. Wrap in waxed paper or plastic wrap. Chill in refrigerator several hours.

Cut rolls in slices, about ¹/₆" thick. Place on greased baking sheet, about 1" apart.

Bake in 350° oven 10 minutes or until done. Remove from baking sheets; cool on racks.

Spread one cookie with Mint Cream Filling. Top with another cookie forming a sandwich cookie. Dip each sandwich cookie in Shiny Chocolate Glaze, so glaze covers half of cookie. Leave other half unglazed. Let glaze dry on racks over waxed paper. If you wish, decorate each cookie with a rosebud and leaf made with your favorite decorating frosting. Makes 2½ dozen.

Mint Cream Filling: Cream together ¼ c. butter or regular margarine and 2 c. sifted confectioners sugar in bowl, using electric mixer at medium speed. Add ⅛ tsp. mint flavoring and 5 tsp. milk; blend well. Add 1 more tsp. milk, if necessary, to make a creamy filling.

Shiny Chocolate Glaze: Melt together 2 (1 oz.) squares unsweetened chocolate and 2 tblsp. butter or regular margarine in saucepan over low heat. Remove from heat. Stir in 2 c. sifted confectioners sugar and 5 tblsp. milk, blending well. Add 1 more tblsp. milk, if necessary, to make a glaze that coats the cookies.

CHOCOLATE LINDER COOKIES

These cookies bake into soft rounded puffs. The inside is cakey and delicately flavored. An Iowa woman freezes batches of these tender little treats to give as Christmas gifts.

2 c. unsifted flour	½ c. shortening
2 tsp. baking powder	2 c. sugar
¼ tsp. salt	4 eggs
4 (1 oz.) squares	2 tsp. vanilla
unsweetened chocolate	Sugar

Stir together flour, baking powder and salt; set aside.

Combine chocolate and shortening in medium saucepan. Cook over low heat until melted. Remove from heat.

Add 2 c. sugar; mix well. Add eggs, one at a time, beating well

97

after each addition. Blend in vanilla. Stir in dry ingredients, mixing well. Chill mixture in refrigerator 2 to 3 hours.

Shape mixture in 1" balls. Roll in sugar. Place on lightly greased baking sheets, about 2" apart.

Bake in 375° oven 9 to 10 minutes or until done. Remove from baking sheets; cool on racks. Makes 6 dozen.

BLACK WALNUT/CHOCOLATE COOKIES

"If you like black walnuts, you'll love this extra crisp cookie," a Kansas farm woman told us. "I've been baking them for 25 years and they are still my favorite cookie to serve with coffee."

2½ c. unsifted flour	½ tsp. black walnut flavoring
2 tsp. baking powder	2 (1 oz.) squares
½ tsp. salt	unsweetened chocolate,
½ c. shortening	melted and cooled
1½ c. sugar	¼ c. milk
1 egg	½ c. chopped black walnuts
1 tsp. vanilla	

Stir together flour, baking powder and salt; set aside.

Cream together shortening and sugar in bowl until light and fluffy, using electric mixer at medium speed. Add egg, vanilla, walnut flavoring and cooled chocolate; blend well.

Add dry ingredients alternately with milk to creamed mixture, mixing well after each addition. Stir in black walnuts. Form dough into 2 rolls, 8" long and 2" in diameter. Wrap in waxed paper or plastic wrap. Chill in refrigerator several hours.

Cut in ¼" slices. Place slices on lightly greased baking sheets, about 2" apart.

Bake in 350° oven 10 minutes or until done. Immediately remove from baking sheets; cool on racks. Makes 5 dozen.

CHOCO-MINT SNAPS

Looks like a chocolate gingersnap—all crackly on the surface. Not only does a Nebraska homemaker make these for her youngster, she uses them to make an extra special chocolate cookie crust for pies.

1¾ c. unsifted flour	1 (6 oz.) pkg. semisweet
2 tsp. baking soda	chocolate pieces,
1 tsp. ground cinnamon	melted and cooled
¼ tsp. salt	¼ c. light corn syrup
⅔ c. shortening	¼ tsp. peppermint extract
½ c. sugar	Sugar
1 egg	

Stir together flour, baking soda, cinnamon and salt; set aside.

Cream together shortening and ½ c. sugar in bowl until light and fluffy, using electric mixer at medium speed. Add egg, cooled chocolate, corn syrup and peppermint extract; blend well.

Stir in dry ingredients, mixing well. Shape mixture into balls, using 1 tblsp. dough for each. Roll in sugar. Place on ungreased baking sheets, about 2" apart.

Bake in 350° oven 10 minutes or until done. Remove from baking sheets; cool on racks. Makes 2½ dozen.

CHOCOLATE REFRIGERATOR COOKIES

Make and chill these cookies in the morning and bake at your convenience. A crackly-crisp cookie with a robust chocolate flavor. (See photo, Plate 5.)

2 c. sifted flour	2 (1 oz.) squares
2 tsp. baking powder	unsweetened chocolate,
½ tsp. salt	melted and cooled
½ c. shortening	⅓ c. milk
1½ c. sugar	½ c. chopped pecans
2 eggs	Sifted confectioners sugar
2 tsp. vanilla	

Sift together flour, baking powder and salt; set aside.

Cream together shortening and sugar in bowl until light and fluffy, using electric mixer at medium speed. Add eggs, one at a time, beating well after each addition. Blend in vanilla and cooled chocolate.

Add dry ingredients alternately with milk, beating well after each addition. Stir in pecans. Cover and chill in refrigerator 3 hours or until mixture holds shape.

Shape into 1" balls, using lightly greased hands. Roll in confectioners sugar. Place on greased baking sheets, about 2" apart.

Bake in 350° oven 14 minutes or until a slight imprint remains on surface of cookie when touched lightly with fingertip. Remove from baking sheets; cool on racks. Makes 6 dozen.

Batches of Brownies

We know that brownies are considered a bar cookie, but we received so many absolutely scrumptious recipes that we decided to devote a whole chapter of this book to farm women's favorite brownie recipes.

Brownie lovers, we found, are divided into two camps: those who think a brownie must be very moist, very fudgy and extra-rich and those who like a brownie that is tender-crumbed and cake-like in texture. We have plenty of recipes in both categories as well as a Homemade Brownie Mix so that you can stir up a batch of brownies in minutes.

For the extra fudgies, try Rocky Road Brownies, which are deliciously bumpy with marshmallows and nuts. Or tempt your family with a pan of deep dark delicious Chewy Fudge Brownies, a cross between a candy and a brownie.

Planning a bake sale? Be sure to take a batch of Chocolate Peppermint Bars or Toasted Marshmallow Brownies.

Whatever brownie recipe you decide to try first, for whatever occasion, we think that they will disappear fast, fast, fast.

BROWNIES WITH BROWNED BUTTER FROSTING

Buttery icing drizzled with spiders of chocolate. This moist chewy brownie with its contrasting frosting comes to us from a Nebraska woman who says she received it from a friend years ago. (See photo, Plate 5.)

1 c. butter or regular margarine	1¼ c. sifted flour
4 (1 oz.) squares unsweetened chocolate	1 c. chopped pecans
2 c. sugar	Browned Butter Frosting (recipe follows)
4 eggs	½ (1 oz.) square unsweetened chocolate
1 tsp. vanilla	

Combine butter and 4 oz. chocolate in small saucepan. Cook over low heat until butter and chocolate are melted. Remove from heat; cool to room temperature.

Beat together sugar and eggs in large mixing bowl 2 minutes, using electric mixer at high speed. Blend in cooled chocolate mixture and vanilla. Stir in flour; mix well. Stir in pecans. Spread mixture in greased 13x9x2" baking pan.

Bake in 350° oven 35 minutes or until brownies test done. Cool in pan on rack. Frost with Browned Butter Frosting.

Melt ½ oz. unsweetened chocolate in custard cup in hot, but not boiling water. Drizzle over frosting. Let stand until chocolate sets. Cut into 2" squares. Makes 24 brownies.

Browned Butter Frosting: Melt ¼ c. butter in small saucepan over low heat. Continue heating, stirring constantly, until delicately browned. Remove from heat. Combine 2 c. sifted confectioners sugar, 2 tblsp. light cream and 1 tsp. vanilla in bowl. Add browned butter. Beat with electric mixer at medium speed until smooth and creamy.

CHOCOLATE MARBLED BROWNIES

"A treasured secret recipe for years. My husband begs me to make them. My friends ask me to bring them as a birthday present. At my husband's urging, I am sending you the recipe as he feels it's not fair not to share such a good recipe." —*A New York homemaker.*

1⅓ c. sifted flour
1 tsp. baking powder
½ tsp. salt
⅔ c. butter or
   regular margarine
2 c. sugar
4 eggs
4 (1 oz.) envs. unsweetened
   liquid chocolate
2 tsp. vanilla
1 c. chopped walnuts

2 (3 oz.) pkgs. cream
   cheese, softened
⅓ c. butter or
   regular margarine
⅓ c. sugar
2 tblsp. flour
2 eggs
¾ tsp. vanilla
Easy Chocolate Frosting
   (recipe follows)

Sift together 1⅓ c. flour, baking powder and salt; set aside.

Cream together ⅔ c. butter and 2 c. sugar in bowl until light and fluffy, using electric mixer at medium speed. Add 4 eggs, one at a time, beating well after each addition. Blend in liquid chocolate and 2 tsp. vanilla. Stir in dry ingredients and walnuts. Set aside.

Beat together cream cheese and ⅓ c. butter in small bowl until smooth, using electric mixer at medium speed. Add ⅓ c. sugar, 2 tblsp. flour, 2 eggs and ¾ tsp. vanilla. Beat until smooth.

Spread one half of chocolate batter in greased 13x9x2" baking pan. Spread cream cheese mixture evenly over all. Spoon remaining chocolate batter over cream cheese layer. Use a metal spatula to swirl layers to give marbled effect.

Bake in 350° oven 40 minutes or until done. Cool in pan on rack. Frost with Easy Chocolate Frosting. Cut into 3x1" bars. Makes 36.

Easy Chocolate Frosting: Combine 2 c. sifted confectioners sugar, 2 (1 oz.) envs. unsweetened liquid chocolate, ¼ c. melted butter or regular margarine, 3 tblsp. milk and 1 tsp. vanilla in bowl. Beat with electric mixer at medium speed until smooth and creamy.

HOMEMADE BROWNIE MIX

"Here's a recipe for Brownie Mix that my mother sent to me," said an Iowa woman. "I just love it because it's so convenient to have on hand—in practically minutes, I can make a batch of brownies."

4 c. sifted flour	**1½ c. nonfat dry milk**
4½ c. sugar	**1½ tblsp. baking powder**
1 c. baking cocoa	**1½ tsp. salt**

Sift together flour, sugar, cocoa, dry milk, baking powder and salt three times. Store in airtight container.

To Make Brownies: Combine 1¾ c. Homemade Brownie Mix, 1 egg, ¼ c. warm water, ¼ c. cooking oil and 1 tsp. vanilla in bowl. Beat with electric mixer 1 minute at medium speed. Stir in ¼ c. chopped walnuts. Pour into greased 9" square baking pan. Bake in 350° oven 20 minutes or until brownies are done. Cool in pan on rack. Cut into 2" squares. Makes 16.

ROCKY ROAD BARS

Super-rich, layered brownies spread with a luscious chocolate cream cheese frosting. "My family prefers this brownie to a box of candy," said a Wisconsin farm wife.

½ c. butter or regular margarine	¼ c. butter or regular margarine
1 (1 oz.) square unsweetened chocolate	½ c. sugar
1 c. sifted flour	1 egg
1 tsp. baking powder	½ tsp. vanilla
2 eggs	2 tblsp. flour
1 c. sugar	¼ c. chopped walnuts
1 tsp. vanilla	1 (6 oz.) pkg. semisweet chocolate pieces
½ c. chopped walnuts	2 c. miniature marshmallows
1 (8 oz.) pkg. cream cheese, softened	Chocolate Cream Cheese Frosting (recipe follows)

Combine ½ c. butter and 1 oz. chocolate in small saucepan. Melt over low heat. Remove from heat; cool to room temperature.

Sift together 1 c. flour and baking powder; set aside.

Beat together 2 eggs, 1 c. sugar and 1 tsp. vanilla in bowl. Beat with electric mixer at medium speed 1 minute. Blend in chocolate mixture, beating well.

Add dry ingredients; mix well. Stir in ½ c. walnuts. Spread mixture in greased 13x9x2" baking pan.

Reserve 2 oz. cream cheese for frosting. Place remaining cream cheese in bowl. Cream together cream cheese, ¼ c. butter and ½ c. sugar until light and fluffy, using electric mixer at medium speed. Add 1 egg, ½ tsp. vanilla and 2 tblsp. flour; blend well. Stir in ¼ c. walnuts. Spread over batter. Sprinkle with chocolate pieces.

Bake in 325° oven 35 minutes or until done. Remove from oven. Sprinkle with marshmallows and return to oven for 2 minutes or until marshmallows are softened. Cool in pan on rack. Meanwhile, prepare Chocolate Cream Cheese Frosting. Frost brownies while still warm. Cool completely. Cut into 3x1" bars. Makes 36.

Chocolate Cream Cheese Frosting: Combine 1 (1 oz.) square unsweetened chocolate and ¼ c. butter or regular margarine in saucepan. Cook over low heat until melted. Cool well. Combine reserved 2 oz. cream cheese, softened, ¼ c. milk, 1 tsp. vanilla and 3 c. sifted confectioners sugar and cooled chocolate mixture in bowl. Beat with electric mixer at medium speed until frosting mixture is smooth and creamy.

CHEWY FUDGE BROWNIES

A deep dark delicious treat that is a cross between a brownie and a candy. "A hand-me-down recipe from my mother," wrote an Alabama woman. "I've been making this quick-and-easy dessert for over 40 years."

¼ c. butter or regular margarine	½ c. unsifted self-rising flour
3 (1 oz.) squares unsweetened chocolate	1 tsp. vanilla
1⅓ c. sugar	⅔ c. chopped pecans
2 eggs	

Combine butter and chocolate in small saucepan. Melt over low heat. Remove from heat. Pour mixture into bowl. Add sugar and eggs. Beat with electric mixer at medium speed until well blended. Stir in flour and vanilla. Stir in pecans. Spread mixture in greased 9" square baking pan.

Bake in 325° oven 30 minutes or until done. Cool in pan on rack. Cut into 2" squares while still warm. Makes 16.

CHOCOLATE PEPPERMINT BARS

"Chocolate anything is a top favorite with my husband, daughter and three sons," a Texas woman told us. "My daughter usually prefers cakes and the boys ask for bar cookies. They all voted this recipe—my best." (See photo, Plate 5.)

2 (1 oz.) squares unsweetened chocolate	3 tblsp. butter or regular margarine
½ c. butter or regular margarine	5 tsp. milk
2 eggs	1 tsp. peppermint extract
1 c. sugar	1½ (1 oz.) squares unsweetened chocolate
½ c. sifted flour	1½ tblsp. butter or regular margarine
½ c. chopped toasted almonds	1 tblsp. crushed peppermint candy
1½ c. sifted confectioners sugar	

Combine 2 oz. chocolate and ½ c. butter in saucepan. Cook over low heat until melted. Remove from heat; cool well.

Beat together eggs and sugar in bowl until thick and lemon-colored, using electric mixer at high speed. Blend in chocolate mixture and flour. Beat until smooth. Stir in almonds. Spread in greased 8" square baking pan.

Bake in 350° oven 25 minutes or until toothpick inserted in center comes out clean. Cool in pan on rack.

Combine confectioners sugar, 3 tblsp. butter, milk and peppermint extract in bowl. Beat with electric mixer at medium speed until smooth. Spread on cooled brownies. Cover and chill in refrigerator until cream layer is firm.

Melt 1½ oz. chocolate with 1½ tblsp. butter over hot water. Cool slightly and spread carefully over cream layer. Sprinkle with peppermint candy. Cut into 2x1" bars. Makes 32.

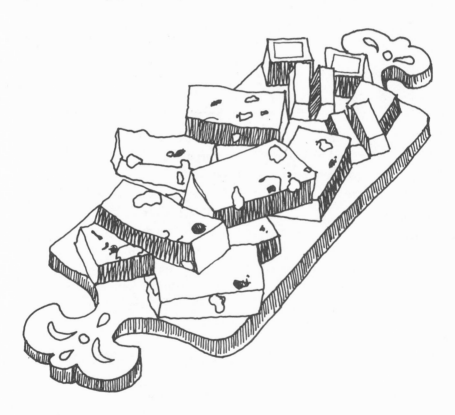

PECAN BROWNIES

If you want to go on a brownie binge, try this recipe—it makes two full pans of rich, fudgy, chewy brownies loaded with pecan halves. A Nebraska woman adapted this recipe from one she found in a New York pastry shop. Worth every calorie.

2 c. sugar	6 (1 oz.) squares
1 c. brown sugar, packed	unsweetened chocolate,
⅔ c. light corn syrup	melted and cooled
1 c. butter or regular	2 c. sifted flour
margarine	2 c. pecan halves
6 eggs	

Combine sugar, brown sugar, corn syrup and butter in large mixing bowl. Beat with electric mixer at medium speed for 2 minutes or until smooth.

Add eggs; beat 2 more minutes. Blend in cooled chocolate.

Add flour; stir well. Reserve 32 pecan halves for decoration. Stir in remaining pecans. Spread batter evenly in 2 greased 9" square baking pans. Arrange 16 reserved pecan halves in rows on top in each pan.

Bake in 350° oven 40 minutes or until done. Cool in pans on racks. Cut each pan into 16 (2") squares. Makes 32.

DELUXE BROWNIE FINGERS

Make them in a saucepan and bake in a jelly roll pan. An Iowa woman wrote us, "Every farm woman should have a recipe this easy, fast and good—only two pans to wash up. I found the recipe in a boxful of old recipes in the attic when we bought our house years ago. I can't tell you how many times I have written out this recipe for friends and neighbors."

¼ c. baking cocoa	1 tsp. baking soda
1 c. butter or regular	2 eggs
margarine	1 tsp. vanilla
1 c. water	½ c. buttermilk
2 c. sifted flour	Fudge Frosting
2 c. sugar	(recipe follows)

Combine cocoa, butter and water in 3-qt. saucepan. Cook over medium heat, stirring constantly, until butter is melted. Remove from heat; cool slightly.

Sift together flour, sugar and baking soda. Stir dry ingredients into chocolate mixture, mixing well with wooden spoon. Blend in eggs, vanilla and buttermilk, mixing well. Pour batter into greased 15½x10½x1" jelly roll pan.

Bake in 375° oven 20 minutes or until done. Cool in pan on rack. Frost with Fudge Frosting. Cut into 4x1" bars. Makes 40.

Fudge Frosting: Combine 1½ c. sugar, 6 tblsp. butter or regular margarine, 6 tblsp. milk and ½ c. semisweet chocolate pieces in 2-qt. saucepan. Bring to a boil, stirring constantly. Add 20 miniature marshmallows. Boil 1 minute, stirring constantly. Remove from heat. Cool to lukewarm (120°). Beat with electric mixer at medium speed until frosting is of spreading consistency.

FRIENDSHIP BROWNIES

An Iowa farm woman sent us this recipe and said, "The recipe originally belonged to a dear neighbor who could always be counted on to bake brownies for a shut-in, college youngsters, servicemen and birthday gifts. Now I make them for my family and share them with my friends. Everyone looks forward to these treats."

1½ c. sifted flour	2 c. sugar
½ c. baking cocoa	4 eggs
1 tsp. baking powder	2 tsp. vanilla
1 tsp. salt	1 c. chopped walnuts
⅔ c. butter or	Sifted confectioners sugar
regular margarine	

Sift together flour, cocoa, baking powder and salt; set aside.

Cream together butter and sugar in bowl until light and fluffy, using electric mixer at medium speed. Add eggs, one at a time, beating well after each addition. Blend in vanilla.

Stir in dry ingredients, stirring well after each addition. Stir in walnuts. Spread in greased 13x9x2" baking pan.

Bake in 350° oven 30 minutes or until done. Cool pan on rack. Dust with confectioners sugar. Cut into 2" squares. Makes 24.

DOUBLE BOILER BROWNIES

"We like this recipe because it uses plenty of eggs from our farm and because it can be mixed from start to finish in a deep double boiler. And last, but not least—it's chocolatey!" wrote a Wisconsin woman.

4 (1 oz.) squares	1 tsp. salt
unsweetened chocolate	2 c. sugar
⅔ c. cooking oil	4 eggs
1½ c. sifted flour	1 c. chopped walnuts
1 tsp. baking powder	Sifted confectioners sugar

Combine chocolate and oil in top of double boiler. Place over simmering water until chocolate is melted. Remove from heat.

Sift together flour, baking powder and salt; set aside.

Blend sugar into chocolate mixture, using electric mixer at medium speed. Add eggs; beat 2 minutes.

Add dry ingredients and mix well. Stir in walnuts. (Batter is stiff.) Spread mixture in greased 15½x10½x1" jelly roll pan.

Bake in 350° oven 25 minutes or until done. Cool in pan on rack. Dust with confectioners sugar. Cut into 4x1" bars. Makes 40.

CHOCOLATE CREAM CHEESE BARS

A two-tone brownie that sells out in minutes at bake sales. Make a big batch to tote to picnics or to serve to guests a la mode with ice cream and chocolate sauce.

½ c. butter or	¾ c. chopped walnuts
regular margarine	1 (8 oz.) pkg. cream cheese,
1 (1 oz.) square	softened
unsweetened chocolate	¼ c. butter or regular
1 c. sifted flour	margarine
1 c. sugar	½ c. sugar
1 tsp. baking powder	2 tblsp. flour
¼ tsp. salt	1 egg, beaten
2 eggs, beaten	½ tsp. vanilla
1 tsp. vanilla	¼ c. chopped walnuts

Combine ½ c. butter and chocolate in 2-qt. saucepan. Cook over low heat until butter and chocolate are melted. Remove from heat; cool to room temperature.

Sift together 1 c. flour, 1 c. sugar, baking powder and salt. Stir dry ingredients into cooled chocolate mixture; mix well. Add 2 eggs and 1 tsp. vanilla, blending well. Stir in ¾ c. walnuts. Spread batter in well-greased 13x9x2" baking pan.

Combine cream cheese and ¼ c. butter in bowl. Beat until smooth and creamy, using electric mixer. Combine ½ c. sugar and 2 tblsp. flour. Add to cheese mixture, beating well. Beat in 1 egg and ½ tsp. vanilla. Spread over batter. Sprinkle with ¼ c. walnuts.

Bake in 350° oven 30 to 35 minutes or until done. Cool in pan on rack. Cut into 3x1" bars. Makes 24.

TRI-LEVEL BROWNIES

All three layers are scrumptious when you bite down through this brownie. The foundation is a crisp butterscotchy oatmeal crust topped with a moist brownie layer and iced with a satiny dark chocolate fudge frosting.

½ c. sifted flour	⅔ c. sifted flour
¼ tsp. baking soda	¼ tsp. baking powder
¼ tsp. salt	¼ tsp. salt
½ c. brown sugar, packed	¾ c. sugar
1 c. quick-cooking oats	1 egg
6 tblsp. melted butter or regular margarine	¼ c. milk
	½ tsp. vanilla
1 (1 oz.) square unsweetened chocolate	½ c. chopped walnuts
¼ c. butter or regular margarine	Fudge Frosting (recipe follows)

Sift together ½ c. flour, baking soda and ¼ tsp. salt into mixing bowl. Add brown sugar and oats; mix well. Stir in 6 tblsp. butter. Pat mixture into 9" ungreased baking pan.

Bake in 350° oven 10 minutes. Meanwhile, prepare filling. Melt chocolate and ¼ c. butter in small saucepan over low heat. Remove from heat. Cool slightly.

Sift together ⅔ c. flour, baking powder and ¼ tsp. salt; set aside.

Combine sugar, cooled chocolate mixture and egg. Beat with electric mixer at medium speed 1 minute. Add dry ingredients alternately with milk, beating well after each addition. Blend in vanilla and walnuts. Spread over first layer.

Bake in 350° oven 30 minutes or until done. Cool in pan on rack. Frost with Fudge Frosting. Cut into 1½" squares. Makes 36.

Fudge Frosting: Combine 1 (1 oz.) square unsweetened chocolate and 2 tblsp. butter or regular margarine in small saucepan. Place over low heat until melted. Remove from heat. Cool to room temperature. Combine 1½ c. sifted confectioners sugar, 1 tsp. vanilla, 5 tsp. hot water and chocolate mixture in bowl. Mix until smooth and creamy.

MISSISSIPPI MUD BARS

Don't even try to count the calories—just enjoy every mouthful of these super rich brownies, loaded with coconut and chopped pecans.

1 c. butter or regular margarine	1 (3½ oz.) can flaked coconut
2 c. sugar	1½ c. chopped pecans
¼ c. baking cocoa	1 (7½ oz.) jar marshmallow creme
4 eggs	Cocoa Frosting
1 tsp. vanilla	(recipe follows)
1½ c. sifted flour	

Cream together butter, sugar and cocoa in bowl until light and fluffy, using electric mixer at medium speed. Add eggs and vanilla. Beat 2 more minutes at medium speed.

Blend in flour. Stir in coconut and pecans. Spread mixture in greased 15½x10½x1" jelly roll pan.

Bake in 350° oven 30 minutes or until done. Remove from oven; spoon marshmallow creme over all. Let stand 5 minutes. Spread carefully with metal spatula. Prepare Cocoa Frosting and frost while brownies are still warm. Cool completely. Cut into 4x1" bars. Makes 40.

Cocoa Frosting: Combine ½ c. butter or regular margarine and ½ c. baking cocoa in saucepan. Place over low heat until butter melts. Cool slightly. Combine 4 c. sifted confectioners sugar, ½ c. evaporated milk and 1 tsp. vanilla in bowl. Add cooled cocoa mixture. Beat with electric mixer until smooth.

BLONDE BROWNIES

Excellent! A golden brownie generously studded with chocolate pieces and nuts. Brown sugar makes it taste like butterscotch.

2 c. sifted flour	**1 c. brown sugar, packed**
1 tsp. baking powder	**2 eggs**
¼ tsp. baking soda	**1 tsp. vanilla**
1 tsp. salt	**1 (6 oz.) pkg. semisweet**
½ c. shortening	**chocolate pieces**

Sift together flour, baking powder, baking soda and salt; set dry ingredients aside.

Cream together shortening and brown sugar in bowl until light

115

and fluffy, using electric mixer at medium speed. Add eggs, one at a time, beating well after each addition. Blend in vanilla.

Add dry ingredients, mixing well. Stir in chocolate pieces. (Batter is very stiff.) Spread in greased 8" square baking dish.

Bake in 325° oven 35 minutes or until done. Cool in dish on rack. Cut into 2" squares. Makes 16.

CHOCOLATE CHIP BROWNIES

"The following recipe is easy to whip up in a hurry when you need to take a dessert to a church supper. My mother gave me this timesaver," a Wisconsin woman told us.

1 (18½ oz.) yellow cake mix	¼ c. brown sugar, packed
2 eggs	½ c. semisweet chocolate pieces
¼ c. water	¼ c. chopped walnuts
¼ c. butter or regular margarine	

Combine cake mix, eggs, water, butter and brown sugar in bowl. Beat until smooth, using wooden spoon. Stir in chocolate pieces and walnuts. Spread mixture in greased 15½x10½x1" jelly roll pan.

Bake in 350° oven 25 minutes or until done. Cool in pan on rack. Cut into 2" squares. Makes 35.

GERMAN CHOCOLATE/CHEESE BROWNIES

Farm Journal's testing staff unanimously voted this recipe outstanding. They all liked the crunchy toasted almonds in the batter as well as the whisper of almond extract. An Iowa farm wife selected this as her favorite recipe for any occasion.

2 (4 oz.) pkgs. German sweet chocolate
6 tblsp. butter or regular margarine
2 (3 oz.) pkgs. cream cheese
4 tblsp. butter or regular margarine
½ c. sugar
2 eggs
2 tblsp. flour

1 tsp. vanilla
4 eggs
1½ c. sugar
1 c. sifted flour
1 tsp. baking powder
½ tsp. salt
½ tsp. almond extract
2 tsp. vanilla
1 c. chopped toasted almonds

Combine sweet chocolate and 6 tblsp. butter in 2-qt. saucepan. Place over low heat, stirring occasionally, until melted. Remove from heat; cool to room temperature.

Cream together cream cheese and 4 tblsp. butter in bowl, using electric mixer at medium speed. Add ½ c. sugar, beating until light and fluffy. Blend in 2 eggs, 2 tblsp. flour and 1 tsp. vanilla.

Beat 4 eggs in another mixing bowl until foamy, using electric mixer at high speed. Gradually add 1½ c. sugar, beating until thick and lemon-colored.

Sift together 1 c. flour, baking powder and salt. Add to egg mixture, mixing well. Blend in cooled chocolate mixture, almond extract and vanilla. Stir in almonds. Reserve 2 c. of chocolate batter. Spread remaining chocolate batter in greased 13x9x2" baking pan. Spread cream cheese mixture over first layer. Spoon reserved 2 c. chocolate batter over all. Use a metal spatula to swirl layers to give a marbled effect.

Bake in 350° oven 50 minutes or until done. Cool in pan on rack. Cut into 2" squares. Makes 24.

SEMISWEET CHOCOLATE BROWNIES

A very mild chocolate-flavored brownie for those who like a delicate chocolate flavor with a texture that's in between a cake and fudgy brownie. Dust lightly with confectioners sugar, if you wish.

1½ c. sifted flour	3 (1 oz.) squares
½ tsp. salt	semisweet chocolate,
1 c. butter or regular	melted and cooled
margarine	2 tsp. vanilla
2 c. sugar	1 c. chopped walnuts
4 eggs	

Sift together flour and salt; set aside. Cream together butter and sugar in large mixing bowl until light and fluffy, using electric mixer at medium speed. Add eggs; beat well. Blend in cooled chocolate and vanilla. Stir in walnuts. Pour into greased 13x9x2" baking pan.

Bake in 350° oven 35 minutes or until done. Cool in pan on rack. Cut into 3x1" bars. Makes 36.

BUTTERMILK BROWNIES

A cinnamon-flavored brownie—no nuts in the batter but plenty in the milk chocolate icing. Buttermilk makes this extra-moist.

2 c. sifted flour	1 c. water
2 c. sugar	3 tblsp. baking cocoa
1 tsp. baking soda	½ c. buttermilk
½ tsp. salt	2 eggs
½ tsp. ground cinnamon	1 tsp. vanilla
1 c. butter or regular margarine	Milk Chocolate Frosting (recipe follows)

Sift together flour, sugar, baking soda, salt and cinnamon into mixing bowl.

Combine butter, water and cocoa in saucepan. Place over medium heat until butter melts. Remove from heat.

Add cocoa mixture to dry ingredients. Beat with electric mixer at medium speed for 1 minute. Add buttermilk, eggs and vanilla. Beat 1 more minute at medium speed. (Batter is thin.) Pour batter into greased 15½x10½x1" jelly roll pan.

Bake in 350° oven 25 minutes. Cool in pan on rack. Meanwhile, prepare Milk Chocolate Frosting and frost brownies while they are warm. Cool completely. Cut into 2½x1½" bars. Makes 48.

Milk Chocolate Frosting: Sift 1 (1 lb.) box confectioners sugar into bowl; set aside. Combine ½ c. butter or regular margarine, 6 tblsp. milk and 3 tblsp. baking cocoa in saucepan. Place over me-

119

dium heat until butter melts. Remove from heat. Add to confectioners sugar with 1 tsp. vanilla. Beat with electric mixer at medium speed until smooth. Stir in ½ c. chopped walnuts.

EASY CHOCOLATE BROWNIES

A good basic brownie made with a can of chocolate syrup. The recipe doesn't require many ingredients and is so simple to mix together that even a youngster can make it.

½ c. butter or
   regular margarine
1 c. sugar
4 eggs
1 (1 lb.) can chocolate-
   flavored syrup

1 c. sifted flour
Semisweet Chocolate
   Frosting (recipe
   follows)

Cream together butter and sugar in bowl until light and fluffy, using electric mixer at medium speed. Add eggs, one at a time, beating well after each addition. Blend in syrup. Add flour, beating well. Pour into greased 13x9x2" baking pan.

Bake in 350° oven 30 minutes or until done. Cool in pan on rack. Frost with Semisweet Chocolate Frosting. Cut into 2" squares. Makes 24.

Semisweet Chocolate Frosting: Combine 1⅓ c. sugar, 6 tblsp. milk and 7 tblsp. butter or regular margarine in 2-qt. saucepan. Bring mixture to a boil, stirring constantly. Boil 1 minute. Add ½ c. semisweet chocolate pieces and 1 tsp. vanilla. Stir until chocolate is melted. Set saucepan in bowl filled with iced water. Beat with electric mixer at medium speed until frosting is thickened and of spreading consistency.

COFFEE ICED BROWNIES

Very dark chocolate brownies, chewy and crunchy with nuts. Serve plain with ice cream or frost with Coffee Icing for a special occasion.

⅔ c. sifted flour
¼ c. baking cocoa
2 eggs
1 c. sugar
⅓ c. butter or
   regular margarine

1 tsp. vanilla
½ c. chopped pecans
Coffee Icing
   (recipe follows)

Sift together flour and baking cocoa; set aside.

Beat together eggs and sugar in bowl until thick and lemon-colored, using electric mixer at high speed for 2 minutes. Add butter and vanilla; beat well.

Blend in dry ingredients. Stir in pecans. Spread batter in greased 8" square baking pan.

Bake in 350° oven 25 minutes or until done. Cool in pan on rack. Frost with Coffee Icing. Cut into 2" squares. Makes 16.

Coffee Icing: Combine 1¾ c. sifted confectioners sugar, 1 tblsp. baking cocoa, 1 tblsp. butter or regular margarine, 2 tblsp. strong hot coffee and 1 tsp. vanilla in bowl. Beat with spoon until frosting is smooth.

TOASTED MARSHMALLOW BROWNIES

"These brownies are simply delicious," wrote a Nebraska farm woman. "And best of all , they don't need icing—the marshmallows bake

121

on to form a frosting. My kids call them 'moon brownies' because they think the baked marshmallows look like the surface of the moon."

1 c. sifted flour	2 tsp. vanilla
½ c. baking cocoa	1 c. chopped walnuts
1 c. butter or regular	2 c. miniature marshmallows
margarine	¾ c. semisweet chocolate
2 c. sugar	pieces
4 eggs	

Sift together flour and cocoa; set aside.

Cream together butter and sugar in bowl until light and fluffy, using electric mixer at medium speed. Add eggs, one at a time, beating well after each addition. Blend in vanilla. Stir in dry ingredients and walnuts. Spread mixture in 13x9x2" baking pan. Sprinkle with marshmallows and chocolate pieces.

Bake in 325° oven 55 minutes or until done. Cool in pan on rack. Cut into 2" squares. Makes 24.

CHOCOLATE BROWNIE STICKS

A Wisconsin homemaker has been stirring up this cookie for her family for years. Every year she sends her son a big box filled with chocolate sticks for his birthday—it's always his favorite present.

¾ c. butter or	2 eggs
regular margarine	1 tsp. vanilla
2 (1 oz.) squares	1 c. unsifted flour
unsweetened chocolate	½ c. chopped pecans
1 c. sugar	Sifted confectioners sugar

Combine butter and chocolate in saucepan. Cook over low heat until melted. Remove from heat; cool to room temperature.

Beat together sugar, eggs and vanilla in bowl until light and lemon-colored. Blend in cooled chocolate mixture. Stir in flour; mix well. Stir in pecans. Pour into greased 13x9x2" baking pan.

Bake in 350° oven 15 minutes or until done. Cool in pan on rack. While still warm, cut into 3x1" bars. Cool completely. Dust with confectioners sugar. Makes 36.

CARAMEL CHOCOLATE SQUARES

A wickedly rich brownie with a chewy caramel layer. (See photo, Plate 6.) "These brownies are 'extra good,'" wrote a Kentucky farm woman. "Everyone who tastes them wants the recipe right away." We suggest that you just forget your diet and enjoy every crumb.

1 (14 oz.) bag caramels
⅔ c. evaporated milk
1 (18½ oz.) pkg. Swiss
chocolate cake mix
¾ c. melted butter or
regular margarine

1 (6 oz.) pkg. semisweet
chocolate pieces
1 c. chopped walnuts

Combine caramels and ⅓ c. of the evaporated milk in double boiler top. Cover; place over boiling water. Stir until melted. Keep warm over hot water.

Combine cake mix, butter and remaining ⅓ c. evaporated milk in bowl. Beat with electric mixer at medium speed 2 minutes, scraping bowl occasionally. Spread one half of batter in greased 13x9x2" baking pan.

Bake in 350° oven 6 minutes. Cool 2 minutes. Spread caramel

mixture carefully over baked layer. Sprinkle with chocolate pieces. Stir ½ c. of the walnuts into batter. Drop by spoonfuls over all. Sprinkle with remaining ½ c. walnuts.

Bake in 350° oven 18 minutes. Cool in pan on rack. Cut into 3x1" bars. Makes 36.

CHOCOLATE COCONUT BROWNIES

"A moist, chewy, yummy brownie that I have been baking for my family for over 30 years—we like the milk chocolate flavor and hope you do, too," said a Delaware homemaker.

1½ c. sifted flour	2 c. sugar
½ c. baking cocoa	4 eggs
¼ tsp. salt	2 tsp. vanilla
½ c. butter or regular margarine, melted	1 c. flaked coconut

Sift together flour, cocoa and salt; set aside.

Blend together melted butter and sugar in bowl, using electric

124

mixer at medium speed. Add eggs and vanilla; beat 2 more minutes. Add dry ingredients, beating well. Stir in coconut. Spread mixture in greased 13x9x2" baking pan.

Bake in 350° oven 25 minutes or until done. Cool in pan on rack. Cut into 2" squares. Makes 24.

PUDDING BROWNIES

"These easy pudding mix brownies make a big hit everytime I make them," a Missouri farm wife said.

½ c. sifted flour
¼ tsp. baking powder
1 (4 oz.) pkg. chocolate
    pudding and pie filling
⅓ c. butter or regular
    margarine, melted

2 eggs
⅔ c. sugar
1 tsp. vanilla
½ c. chopped walnuts

Sift together flour and baking powder; set aside.

Combine pudding mix and melted butter in bowl. Add eggs, sugar and vanilla; beat with electric mixer at medium speed.

Add dry ingredients, mixing well. Stir in walnuts. Spread in greased 8" square baking pan.

Bake in 350° oven 40 minutes or until done. Cool in pan on rack. Cut into 2" squares. Makes 16.

1949 BROWNIES

The classic fudge brownie that several Farm Journal editors remembered from their childhood as "the only brownie mother ever made."

It is a favorite of a Missouri farmer, too, for almost 30 years. Don't frost or dust with confectioners sugar—just eat plain with milk.

½ c. butter or	¾ tsp. salt
regular margarine	2 eggs
2 (1 oz.) squares	1 c. sugar
unsweetened chocolate	1 tsp. vanilla
¾ c. sifted flour	1 c. chopped walnuts
½ tsp. baking powder	

Combine butter and chocolate in saucepan. Place over low heat until melted. Remove from heat; cool to room temperature.

Sift together flour, baking powder and salt; set aside.

Beat together eggs and sugar in bowl until thick and lemon-colored, using electric mixer at high speed. Blend in cooled chocolate mixture and vanilla.

Add dry ingredients, mixing well. Stir in walnuts. Pour mixture into greased 8" square baking pan.

Bake in 350° oven 30 minutes or until done. Cool in pan on rack. Cut into 2" squares. Makes 16.

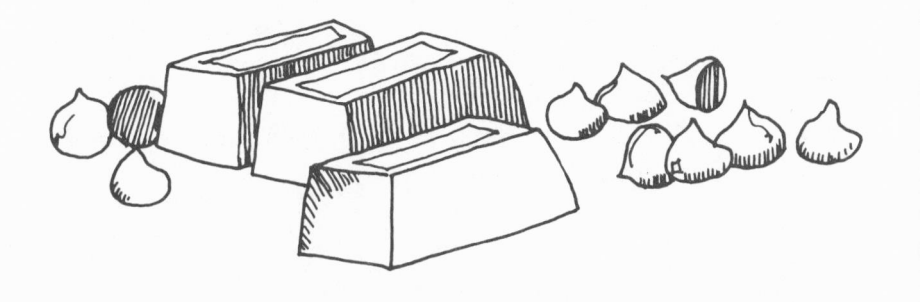

CHEWY COCONUT-CHERRY BROWNIES

"This is an ideal brownie to mail to college youngsters or out-of-town family," wrote an Illinois farm wife. "For mailing, I cut the brownies in small squares and pack in a doily-lined tin container. They make a pretty birthday gift, too."

3 (1 oz.) squares unsweetened chocolate	**1 tsp. vanilla**
½ c. butter or regular margarine	**1 c. sifted flour**
3 eggs	**1 (3½ oz.) can flaked coconut**
¼ tsp. salt	**⅓ c. chopped red maraschino cherries, well drained**
2 c. sugar	

Combine chocolate and butter in small saucepan. Cook over low heat until chocolate and butter are melted. Remove from heat; cool to room temperature.

Combine eggs and salt in mixing bowl. Beat with electric mixer at high speed until foamy. Gradually add sugar, beating until thick and lemon-colored. Blend in cooled chocolate and vanilla. Add flour; stir well to mix. Stir in coconut and maraschino cherries. Pour into greased 13x9x2" baking pan.

Bake in 375° oven 25 minutes or until done. Cool in pan on rack. Cut into 2x1" bars. Makes 36.

RICH PEPPERMINT BROWNIES

A very pretty pale green frosted brownie feathered with bitter chocolate. A refreshing mint flavor comes through both brownie and frost-

ing. These brownies are rich, moist and keep well, according to a Missouri farm wife.

---

1 c. butter or regular margarine	1¾ c. sifted flour 1 tsp. salt
5 (1 oz.) squares unsweetened chocolate	1 c. chopped pecans Peppermint Frosting
5 eggs	(recipe follows)
2¼ c. sugar	½ (1 oz.) square
2 tsp. vanilla	unsweetened chocolate
½ tsp. peppermint extract	

Combine butter and 5 oz. chocolate in saucepan. Place over low heat until melted. Remove from heat; cool to room temperature.

Combine eggs and sugar in mixing bowl. Beat with electric mixer at high speed until light and fluffy, about 2 minutes. Add cooled chocolate mixture, vanilla and peppermint extract; blend well.

Sift together flour and salt. Add dry ingredients to chocolate mixture; mix well. Stir in pecans. Pour into greased 15½x10½x1" jelly roll pan.

Bake in 325° oven 25 minutes or until done. Cool in pan on rack. Frost with Peppermint Frosting.

Melt ½ oz. chocolate in small custard cup in hot water. Drizzle in 5 parallel lines the length of the pan. Gently pull a toothpick across the chocolate lines at even intervals. Let stand until chocolate sets. Cut into 2½x1½" bars. Makes 48.

Peppermint Frosting: Combine 3 c. sifted confectioners sugar, 6 tblsp. cooking oil, 3 tblsp. milk, ½ tsp. peppermint extract and 1 to 2 drops green food color in small mixing bowl. Beat with spoon until smooth and creamy.

A Potpourri of Pies

We have a collection of some of the best chocolate pies that we have ever tasted from great country cooks!

There are several classic chocolate pies, some delicately flavored with chocolate and others with a deep rich flavor. Some are buried under a fluffy meringue or a drift of whipped cream or they are just plain chocolate.

On a cold winter day, bake a Chocolate Pecan Pie or a Chocolate Chess Pie to surprise your family. Or, perhaps they would prefer the Caribbean Fudge Pie that bakes high and puffy and collapses into a creamy fudge center that tastes like a super rich brownie.

There's a medley of refrigerator pies that you can fix in the morning, chill and serve in the evening. Your choices include Chocolate Marshmallow Pie; Chocolate Angel Pie, a gourmet creation nestled in a crisp meringue shell, or Two-Layer Chocolate Pie, which boasts a different and delicious buttery pecan crust.

Select a pie that can be made and frozen for future guests. You'll receive a batch of compliments when you serve Frozen Peppermint Chocolate Pie—it tastes like mousse and ice cream.

Each pie has been tested by a chocolate-loving farm family, and each family says that its pie is the best in the world!

CHOCOLATE ANGEL PIE

A truly gourmet creation you'd expect to find in an elegant restaurant. Three creamy layers are nested in a delicate beige meringue-lined pie shell. "I make several pies and freeze them for a month, providing no one knows they're there," said a South Dakota woman.

Meringue Layer	2 egg yolks, beaten
(recipe follows)	¼ c. water
1 (9") baked pie shell	1 c. heavy cream
1 (6 oz.) pkg. semisweet	¼ c. sugar
chocolate pieces,	¼ tsp. ground cinnamon
melted and cooled	

Prepare Meringue Layer. Spread on bottom and up sides of pie shell. Bake in 325° oven 15 to 18 minutes or until golden brown. Cool on rack.

Combine cooled chocolate, egg yolks and water; beat well with rotary beater or wire whisk. Spread 3 tblsp. of chocolate mixture over Meringue Layer.

Whip heavy cream in bowl until it begins to thicken, using electric mixer at high speed. Gradually add sugar and cinnamon, beating until stiff peaks form. Spread one half of cream mixture over chocolate layer.

Fold remaining chocolate mixture into remaining cream mixture. Spread evenly over cream layer. Cover and refrigerate 4 hours or until set. Makes 6 to 8 servings.

Meringue Layer: Combine 2 egg whites, ½ tsp. vinegar, ¼ tsp. salt and ¼ tsp. ground cinnamon in bowl. Beat with electric mixer at high speed until foamy. Gradually add ½ c. sugar, beating until stiff glossy peaks form.

MARBLED CHOCOLATE RUM PIE

A swirled beauty of pale chocolate and white. Tastes like a mousse or, as one Farm Journal staff member suggested, chocolate and vanilla ice cream.

1 env. unflavored gelatin	1 (12 oz.) pkg. semisweet chocolate pieces
¼ c. sugar	½ c. sugar
⅛ tsp. salt	1 c. heavy cream
1 c. milk	¼ c. sugar
2 eggs, separated	1 tsp. vanilla
¼ c. light rum	1 (9") baked pie shell

Combine gelatin, ¼ c. sugar and salt in top of a double boiler. Add milk, egg yolks and rum. Beat with rotary beater until smooth. Cook over simmering water, stirring constantly, until slightly thickened (about 7 minutes). Remove from heat. Stir in chocolate pieces until melted. Refrigerate until thickened.

Beat egg whites in bowl until foamy, using electric mixer at high speed. Gradually add ½ c. sugar, beating until stiff peaks form. Fold in chocolate mixture.

Whip heavy cream in bowl until it begins to thicken, using electric mixer at high speed. Gradually add ¼ c. sugar and vanilla, beating until stiff peaks form.

Alternate spoonfuls of chocolate mixture and whipped cream in pie shell. Swirl with a spoon to give marbled effect. Refrigerate until set. Makes 6 to 8 servings.

TWO-LAYER CHOCOLATE PIE

"My first-choice pie to make for carry-in dinners, bridal showers, new neighbors and, of course, my family," wrote an Illinois farm woman. The buttery crust, full of pecans, makes it extraordinary.

Pecan Pie Crust
  (recipe follows)
1 (8 oz.) pkg. cream
  cheese, softened
1 c. sifted confectioners
  sugar

1 tsp. vanilla
1 c. heavy cream,
  whipped
1 (5¼ oz.) pkg.
  chocolate pudding and
  pie filling mix

Prepare Pecan Pie Crust.

Combine cream cheese, confectioners sugar and vanilla in bowl. Beat with electric mixer until smooth and creamy. Fold cream cheese mixture into whipped cream. Spread one half of mixture in Pecan Pie Crust. Refrigerate pie as well as remaining cream cheese mixture while preparing chocolate pudding.

Prepare chocolate pudding according to package directions for pie filling. Cool completely. Spread over cream cheese layer. Cover with plastic wrap; refrigerate until set, about 3 hours.

Top with mounds of remaining cream cheese mixture before serving. If you wish, decorate with chocolate shavings. (Just use a vegetable peeler with semisweet chocolate.) Makes 6 to 8 servings.

Pecan Pie Crust: Place 1 c. sifted flour in bowl. Cut in ½ c. butter or regular margarine, using pastry blender. Mix until crumbs form. Stir in 1 c. chopped pecans. Press mixture into lightly greased 9" pie plate. Bake in 350° oven 25 minutes or until lightly browned. Cool on rack.

DIVINE TRIPLE CHOCOLATE PIE

"Every now and then, I'll try a different chocolate pie," a Texas woman wrote, "but my family very firmly tells me it just doesn't compare to my triple chocolate pie." She bakes several pies every year on her Dad's birthday and invites everyone over to celebrate.

Chocolate Pie Shell
  (recipe follows)
1 env. unflavored
  gelatin
1 c. milk
¼ c. sugar
¼ tsp. salt
3 eggs, separated
3 (1 oz.) squares
  unsweetened chocolate

½ tsp. vanilla
¼ tsp. cream of tartar
¼ c. sugar
2 c. heavy cream
2 tblsp. sugar
1 tsp. vanilla
½ (1 oz.) square
  semisweet chocolate

Prepare Chocolate Pie Shell.

Soften gelatin in milk in saucepan 5 minutes.

Blend in ¼ c. sugar, salt and egg yolks; mix well. Add 3 squares unsweetened chocolate. Cook over low heat, stirring constantly, until chocolate is melted and mixture is slightly thickened. (Do not boil.) Pour chocolate mixture into large bowl. Stir in ½ tsp. vanilla. Refrigerate until mixture mounds slightly when dropped from a spoon.

Beat egg whites and cream of tartar in bowl until foamy, using electric mixer at high speed. Gradually beat in ¼ c. sugar, 1 tblsp. at a time, until stiff peaks form.

Beat 1 c. of the heavy cream in another bowl until stiff peaks form, using electric mixer at high speed.

Beat cooled chocolate mixture until smooth. Fold in egg white

133

mixture and whipped cream. Turn into Chocolate Pie Shell. Cover and refrigerate 2 hours or until set.

Beat remaining 1 c. heavy cream in bowl until it begins to thicken, using electric mixer at high speed. Gradually beat in 2 tblsp. sugar and 1 tsp. vanilla.

Decorate pie with puffs of whipped cream mixture. Grate semisweet chocolate over puffs of cream. Makes 6 to 8 servings.

Chocolate Pie Shell: Sift together 1 c. sifted flour and ¼ tsp. salt in bowl. Cut in ⅓ c. shortening until crumbs form. Add ½ (1 oz.) square semisweet chocolate, grated, and 2 tblsp. cold water. Mix lightly until dough holds together. Roll out on floured surface to 12" circle. Line 9" pie plate with dough. Make a fluted rim. Prick with fork. Bake in 400° oven 12 minutes or until done.

CHOCOLATE/MARSHMALLOW PIE

"Our special Sunday pie, especially on a hot summer day," said an Oklahoma woman. "It's cool and refreshing with just the right amount of chocolate. It's a revised edition of my mother's recipe."

30 large marshmallows	**1 (1 oz.) square**
½ c. milk	**unsweetened chocolate**
1 c. heavy cream,	**1 (9") graham cracker**
whipped	**crust**

Combine marshmallows and milk in top of double boiler. Place over simmering water until melted. Stir well. Cool well.

Fold marshmallow mixture into whipped cream. Coarsely grate chocolate, using medium blade. Fold chocolate into cream mixture. Turn into graham cracker crust. Cover and refrigerate 2 hours or until set. Makes 6 to 8 servings.

CHOCOLATE CHIFFON PIE

A creamy textured pie with a good strong chocolate flavor, this light-as-air dessert is a two-generation party favorite from Texas. Perfect ending to a substantial company meal.

1 env. unflavored gelatin	3 eggs, separated
3 tblsp. cold water	1 tsp. vanilla
1 (6 oz.) pkg. semisweet	¼ tsp. cream of tartar
chocolate pieces	⅓ c. sugar
½ c. milk	1 (9") baked pie shell
⅓ c. sugar	with fluted edge
½ tsp. salt	Sweetened whipped cream
1 c. milk	Chocolate jimmies

Soften gelatin in cold water 5 minutes; set aside.

Melt chocolate pieces in ½ c. milk in 2-qt. saucepan over low heat. Stir until smooth. Remove from heat. Stir in ⅓ c. sugar, salt, 1 c. milk and beaten egg yolks. Return to low heat. Cook, stirring constantly, until thick. Stir in gelatin mixture and vanilla. Pour into bowl; refrigerate until mixture mounds slightly when dropped from spoon.

Beat egg whites with cream of tartar in another bowl until frothy, using electric mixer at high speed. Gradually add ⅓ c. sugar, beating until stiff peaks form. Fold in chilled chocolate mixture. Turn mixture into pie shell. Cover with plastic wrap. Refrigerate at least 1 hour or until set. Serve topped with puffs of sweetened whipped cream and sprinkle puffs with chocolate jimmies. Makes 6 to 8 servings.

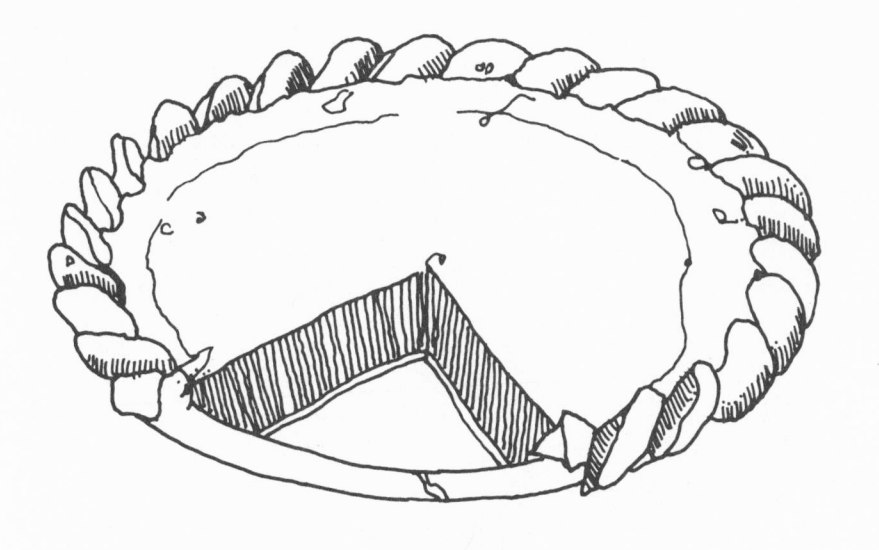

FRENCH CHOCOLATE PIE

Extra-smooth, rich and elegant and unbelievably easy to put together. A Missouri farmer rates this pie best he's ever tasted.

½ c. butter or regular
   margarine, softened
¾ c. sugar
2 (1 oz.) squares
   unsweetened chocolate,
   melted and cooled

2 eggs
2 c. frozen whipped
   topping, thawed
1 (9") baked graham
   cracker crust

Combine butter, sugar and cooled chocolate in large mixing bowl. Beat with electric mixer at medium speed until well blended, about 1 to 2 minutes. Beat in eggs, one at a time, beating well after each addition. Fold in whipped topping. Pour into graham cracker crust. Chill in refrigerator 4 hours or until set. Makes 6 to 8 servings.

136

CHOCOLATE ORANGE MERINGUE PIE

If you always choose chocolate-covered orange creams from a candy box, you'll love this pie. Our testing staff had no comments while sampling—they were too busy eating. The final vote—a heavenly pie!

Meringue Shell	2 tblsp. orange juice
(recipe follows)	1 tblsp. lemon juice
½ c. sugar	1 c. heavy cream
½ tsp. salt	2 (1 oz.) milk
4 egg yolks, beaten	chocolate bars

Prepare Meringue Shell.

Combine sugar, salt, egg yolks, orange juice and lemon juice in small saucepan. Cook over low heat, stirring constantly, until mixture thickens. Remove from heat. Cool completely.

Whip heavy cream in bowl until stiff peaks form, using electric mixer at high speed. Set aside.

Grate 1 chocolate bar into cooled Meringue Shell. Spread one half of whipped cream evenly on top. Cover with cooled filling. Top with remaining whipped cream. Grate remaining chocolate bar and sprinkle on top. Cover and refrigerate 8 hours or overnight. Makes 6 to 8 servings.

Meringue Shell: Beat 4 egg whites in bowl until foamy, using electric mixer at high speed. Add ¼ tsp. cream of tartar. Gradually add ¾ c. sugar, beating until stiff glossy peaks form. Spread meringue into bottom and up sides of well-greased 9" pie plate. Bake in 275° oven 1 hour or until light beige color and crisp to the touch. Turn off heat and leave shell in oven with door open 30 more minutes. Remove from oven and cool on rack.

CREAMY CHOCO-NUT PIE

Pretty-as-a-picture pie with a velvety smooth texture and very subtle chocolate flavor. An easy-to-fix make-ahead company dessert.

1 env. unflavored	1 tsp. vanilla
gelatin	1 c. heavy cream
1½ c. milk	1 (9") baked pie shell
½ c. sugar	with fluted edge
⅛ tsp. salt	Sweetened whipped cream
1 (6 oz.) pkg. semisweet	Walnut halves
chocolate pieces	

Soften gelatin in milk in 2-qt. saucepan 5 minutes.

Add sugar, salt and chocolate pieces. Cook over medium heat, stirring constantly, until chocolate is melted. Remove from heat; pour into bowl. Beat with rotary beater until mixture is smooth. Stir in vanilla. Refrigerate until mixture mounds slightly when dropped from spoon.

Whip heavy cream in bowl until stiff peaks form, using electric mixer at high speed. Fold in thickened chocolate mixture. Turn into pie shell. Cover and refrigerate 3 hours or until set.

Decorate with sweetened whipped cream puffs and walnut halves. Makes 6 to 8 servings.

FLUFFY CHOCOLATE PIE

"A recipe that dates back to the flappers and jazz era of the 20's," a *North Carolina woman informed us in a letter. A lovely pie with a cloud-like texture.*

1 c. evaporated milk
1 env. unflavored
   gelatin
¼ c. cold water
¾ c. sugar
½ c. milk
⅛ tsp. salt
1 egg yolk, beaten
3 (1 oz.) squares
   unsweetened chocolate,
   melted and cooled

1 tsp. vanilla
1 (9") baked pie shell
1 c. heavy cream
2 tblsp. sugar
1 tsp. vanilla
½ (1 oz.) square
   semisweet chocolate,
   melted and cooled

Pour evaporated milk into freezer tray. Freeze until partially frozen around edges. Meanwhile, chill small bowl and beaters.

Meanwhile, soften gelatin in cold water; set aside.

Combine ¾ c. sugar, milk and salt in top of double boiler. Cook over simmering water until milk is hot and sugar is dissolved. Stir some of hot mixture into egg yolk. Then stir all of egg yolk mixture into hot milk mixture. Cook, stirring constantly, over simmering water 2 minutes. Stir in softened gelatin, 3 squares cooled chocolate and 1 tsp. vanilla. Remove from heat. Chill mixture in refrigerator until it thickens and mounds slightly when dropped from spoon.

Whip partially frozen evaporated milk in chilled bowl until stiff peaks form, using electric mixer at high speed. Fold chocolate mixture into whipped milk. Pile mixture into baked pie shell. Cover and refrigerate 2 hours or until set.

139

Whip heavy cream in bowl until it begins to thicken. Gradually add 2 tblsp. sugar and 1 tsp. vanilla, beating until soft peaks form. Spread whipped cream over top of pie. Chill.

Drizzle ½ oz. cooled semisweet chocolate over whipped cream. Chill until serving time. Makes 6 to 8 servings.

GERMAN CHOCOLATE MALLOW PIE

Light-as-air chiffon pie that an Iowa woman has been making for more than 15 years for special occasions. A boon to a busy home-maker as it's simple to make and only requires three hours to chill in the refrigerator until it's set and ready to serve.

2 oz. German sweet chocolate (½ bar)	1 tsp. vanilla
35 large marshmallows	1 (9") graham cracker crust
¾ c. milk	Sweetened whipped cream
1 c. heavy cream	Chocolate curls

Combine German chocolate, marshmallows and milk in top of double boiler. Place over simmering water. Heat until melted, stirring occasionally. Remove from heat; cool well.

Whip heavy cream with vanilla in bowl until stiff peaks form, using electric mixer at high speed. Fold chocolate mixture into whipped cream. Pour into graham cracker crust. Cover and refrigerate until set, about 3 hours.

Decorate with sweetened whipped cream and chocolate curls. Makes 6 to 8 servings.

BAVARIAN MINT PIE

Two types of chocolate laced with peppermint flavoring produces a wickedly rich, deep dark pie. "Don't garnish with whipped cream," advised the Minnesota farm woman who sent in the recipe. "Cut into 'teeny' pieces—it's so rich, that's all you can eat."

½ c. butter or
    regular margarine
¾ c. sugar
3 eggs
2 (1 oz.) squares
    unsweetened chocolate,
    melted and cooled

1 (4 oz.) pkg. German
    sweet chocolate, melted
    and cooled
¼ tsp. peppermint flavoring
Vanilla Wafer Crust
    (recipe follows)
¼ c. chopped pecans

Cream together butter and sugar in bowl until light and fluffy, using electric mixer at high speed. Beat in eggs, one at a time, beating well after each addition. Blend in cooled unsweetened chocolate, German chocolate and peppermint flavoring. Turn into Vanilla Wafer Crust. Sprinkle with pecans. Cover and refrigerate until set, about 3 hours. Makes 12 servings.

Vanilla Wafer Crust: Combine 1⅓ c. vanilla wafer crumbs, ¼ c. sugar and 4 tblsp. melted butter or regular margarine in bowl. Mix well. Press crumb mixture into 9" pie plate. Bake in 375° oven 5 minutes. Cool on rack.

CHOCOLATE RUM PIE

"My son-in-law loves all pies as long as they are chocolate," a Washington woman wrote. "I developed this recipe for him—the toasted almonds on the bottom crust make a big hit."

1 (5½ oz.) pkg. chocolate pudding and pie filling mix	⅔ c. toasted slivered almonds
2 c. milk	1 (9") baked pie shell
1 c. heavy cream	4 tsp. sugar
	¼ tsp. rum flavoring

Cook pudding mix according to package directions for pie filling, but using only 2 c. milk. (Filling will be thick.) Remove from heat; pour into bowl. Cover with plastic wrap. Cool well.

Whip ⅓ c. of the heavy cream in bowl until stiff peaks form, using electric mixer at high speed. Fold whipped cream into chocolate mixture.

Remove 3 tblsp. almonds; set aside. Arrange remaining almonds in bottom of pie shell. Add chocolate filling. Cover and refrigerate until set.

Just before serving, whip remaining heavy cream in bowl until it begins to thicken, using electric mixer at high speed. Gradually add sugar and rum flavoring, beating until soft peaks form. Spread whipped cream over top of pie. Decorate with remaining 3 tblsp. almonds. Makes 6 to 8 servings.

CREAMY CHOCOLATE PIE

An ultra-rich cream pie with a quivery, gentle set. A Kansas woman got the recipe from a superior pie maker. "Some folks like a firmly set pie," she wrote, "but we like it on the soft side."

2 (1 oz.) squares unsweetened chocolate	2 tblsp. butter or regular margarine
3 c. milk	1 tsp. vanilla
1 c. sugar	1 (9") baked pie shell
⅓ c. flour	Sweetened whipped cream
¼ tsp. salt	Grated semisweet chocolate
3 egg yolks	

Combine unsweetened chocolate and milk in saucepan. Cook over medium heat until chocolate is melted.

Combine sugar, flour and salt in small bowl. Pour some of hot milk into sugar/flour mixture; beat until smooth. Then stir into remaining hot milk mixture. Cook over medium heat, stirring constantly, until mixture thickens.

Beat egg yolks slightly in bowl. Pour some of hot mixture into egg yolks, blending well. Add egg mixture to hot mixture. Cook over low heat 2 minutes. Remove from heat; add butter and vanilla. Mix until blended. Cool 10 minutes. Pour into pie shell. Cover with plastic wrap. Refrigerate 2 hours or until set.

Spread sweetened whipped cream over top of pie. Decorate with grated semisweet chocolate. Makes 6 to 8 servings.

RICH CHOCOLATE PIE

A very dark, very fudgy, very delicious chocolate cream pie—especially for all those chocolate fans who say, "The stronger the chocolate flavor, the better we like it."

2 (1 oz.) squares unsweetened chocolate	**2 tblsp. butter or regular margarine**
1½ c. milk	**½ tsp. vanilla**
1 c. brown sugar, packed	**1 (9") baked pie shell with fluted rim**
⅓ c. flour	
3 eggs, separated	**6 tblsp. sugar**

Combine chocolate and 1 c. of the milk in 2-qt. heavy saucepan. Cook over medium heat, stirring frequently, until chocolate is melted. Stir in brown sugar.

Combine remaining ½ c. milk with flour in small cup; mix until smooth. Gradually stir into chocolate mixture. Cook over medium heat, stirring constantly, until mixture thickens.

Beat egg yolks slightly. Stir in a little hot mixture into yolks; blend well. Stir yolk mixture into hot mixture. Cook over low heat, stirring constantly, 2 minutes. Remove from heat. Stir in butter and vanilla. Cool 5 minutes. Turn into pie shell.

Beat egg whites in bowl until foamy, using electric mixer at high speed. Gradually add sugar, beating until soft peaks form. Spread meringue over pie filling, sealing edges well.

Bake in 325° oven 12 minutes or until meringue is golden brown. Cool on rack. Makes 6 to 8 servings.

CHOCOLATE MACAROON CREAM PIE

A velvety cream pie crowned with a coconut-flecked meringue that bakes to tawny perfection. One of those dark chocolate pies with a perfect "set"—quivers slightly when cut.

¾ c. sugar	1 tblsp. butter or
3 tblsp. flour	regular margarine
1 tblsp. cornstarch	1 tsp. vanilla
¼ tsp. salt	1 (9") baked pie shell
3 eggs, separated	⅓ c. sugar
1½ c. milk	½ c. flaked coconut
1½ (1 oz.) squares	
unsweetened chocolate,	
melted and cooled	

Combine ¾ c. sugar, flour, cornstarch and salt in top of double boiler. Beat egg yolks slightly. Add egg yolks, milk and cooled

145

chocolate to sugar mixture; mix well. Place over simmering water. Cook 5 minutes, stirring constantly, until thick. Remove from heat. Add butter and vanilla. Stir until blended. Cool 5 minutes. Pour into pie shell.

Beat egg whites until foamy, using electric mixer at high speed. Gradually add ⅓ c. sugar, beating until soft glossy peaks form. Fold in coconut. Top pie with mounds of meringue topping.

Place under broiler, about 10" from source of heat. Broil until delicately browned. Cool on rack. Makes 6 to 8 servings.

GERMAN SWEET CHOCOLATE PIE

Creamy vanilla pudding provides the base for this excellent pie with an unusual crust. "We love this pie because of the crunchy coconut-pecan crust and the light chocolate flavor," wrote an Iowa wife.

⅓ c. butter or
   regular margarine
⅓ c. brown sugar, packed
⅓ c. chopped pecans
⅓ c. flaked coconut
1 (9") baked pie shell
1 (5 oz.) pkg. vanilla
   pudding and pie filling

1 (4 oz.) pkg. German
   sweet chocolate, cut up
2½ c. milk
Sweetened whipped cream
Flaked coconut

Combine butter, brown sugar, pecans and coconut in small saucepan. Cook over medium heat until mixture comes to a boil, stirring frequently. Remove from heat. Cool slightly. Spread in bottom of baked pie shell.

Bake in 450° oven 5 minutes to set filling. Cool well on rack.

Combine pudding mix, sweet chocolate and milk in 2-qt. saucepan. Cook according to package directions for pie filling. Remove from heat; cool 5 minutes. Pour into pie shell. Cover with plastic wrap. Refrigerate 4 hours or until set.

Decorate with puffs of whipped cream and coconut. Makes 6 to 8 servings.

MILK CHOCOLATE PIE

"My husband is a chocolate fan—but it must be milk chocolate," said a California farm woman when she submitted her husband's favorite pie. She often makes and serves the pie filling as a pudding.

¾ c. sugar	½ tsp. vanilla
6 tblsp. cornstarch	1 (9") baked pie shell
2 tblsp. baking cocoa	Sweetened whipped cream
4 c. milk	Walnut halves

Combine sugar, cornstarch and cocoa in top of double boiler. Gradually blend in milk. Cook over hot water until mixture is smooth and thick, stirring occasionally, about 15 minutes. Remove from heat. Stir in vanilla. Cool 5 minutes.

Pour mixture into pie shell. Cover and refrigerate 4 hours or until set. Decorate with puffs of sweetened whipped cream and walnut halves. Makes 6 to 8 servings.

CHOCOLATE CHESS PIE

The English chess pie was popular in American southern plantation kitchens. A Texas woman started with her basic chess pie and ex-

perimented until she came up with this meltingly delicious Chocolate Chess Pie. "My family cheers every time I serve it for dessert," she told us.

---

2 c. sugar	¼ c. milk
2 tblsp. cornstarch	¼ c. butter or regular
4 eggs	margarine, melted
1 (8 oz.) can chocolate-	1 (9") unbaked pie shell
flavored syrup	with fluted edge

Combine sugar, cornstarch, eggs, chocolate-flavored syrup, milk and butter in bowl. Beat with electric mixer at medium speed until smooth, about 1 minute. Pour mixture into pie shell.

Bake in 350° oven 55 minutes or until center is set. Cool on rack. Makes 6 to 8 servings.

CHOCOLATE PECAN PIE

"This will remind you of a regular pecan pie, but we think it's twice as good," a Georgia homemaker told us. "It's so easy to make and fits into any menu. My husband tells me it's a real winner."

¾ c. sugar	3 tblsp. melted butter or
½ tsp. salt	regular margarine
1 c. light corn syrup	3 eggs
3 (1 oz.) squares	1 tsp. vanilla
unsweetened chocolate,	1 c. chopped pecans
melted and cooled	1 (9") unbaked pie shell

Combine sugar, salt, corn syrup, cooled chocolate, butter, eggs and vanilla in bowl. Beat with electric mixer at medium speed until well blended. Stir in pecans. Turn mixture into pie shell.

Bake in 375° oven 35 minutes or until set. (Pie is puffy when it comes out of oven and sinks while cooling.) Cool on rack. Makes 6 to 8 servings.

CHOCOLATE RIPPLE PIE

Another top favorite with our testing staff. Not a crumb left on the plates after the tasting! A three-layered frozen beauty nestled in a rich buttery crust. "Try it—you'll love it," a New York farm wife promised when she sent the recipe.

Butter Crust	**1 egg white**
(recipe follows)	**¼ c. water**
1 (6 oz.) pkg. semisweet	**1 tsp. vanilla**
chocolate pieces	**1 tsp. lemon juice**
¼ c. light corn syrup	**½ c. sugar**
¼ c. water	**1 c. heavy cream, whipped**

Prepare Butter Crust.

Combine chocolate pieces, corn syrup and ¼ c. water in top of double boiler. Cook over simmering water, stirring constantly, until chocolate is melted. Remove from heat; cool well.

Combine egg white, ¼ c. water, vanilla and lemon juice in bowl. Beat with electric mixer at high speed until foamy. Gradually add sugar, beating until soft peaks form (about 4 minutes). Fold whipped cream into egg white mixture. Then fold in two thirds of chocolate mixture.

Spread one half of filling mixture in pie shell. Drizzle with one half of remaining chocolate mixture. Cover with remaining filling. Drizzle remaining chocolate mixture on top in parallel lines. To make rippled effect, pull a knife through filling across lines of

149

chocolate at even intervals. Cover and freeze until firm, about 4 hours. Let stand at room temperature a few minutes before cutting. Makes 6 to 8 servings.

Butter Crust: Combine 1 c. sifted flour and 2 tblsp. sugar in bowl. Cut in ½ c. butter or regular margarine until crumbly, using pastry blender or two knives. Press into 9" pie plate. Bake in 375° oven 13 minutes or until golden brown.

CHOCOLATE CHEESE PIE

Chocolate and cream cheese blend superbly in this velvet-smooth pie. Tastes like softened chocolate ice cream. Best of all, you can make it ahead and refrigerate until you're ready to serve it. It's very rich—you'll want to cut it into small wedges. Definitely not a dessert for dieters. (See photo, Plate 2.)

Chocolate Graham Crust (recipe follows)	**¾ c. light brown sugar, packed**
1 (6 oz.) pkg. semisweet chocolate pieces	**⅛ tsp. salt**
1 (8 oz.) pkg. cream cheese, softened	**1 tsp. vanilla**
	2 eggs, separated
	1 c. heavy cream, whipped

Prepare Chocolate Graham Crust.

Melt chocolate pieces over hot water. Cool 10 minutes.

Blend together cream cheese, ½ c. of the brown sugar, salt and vanilla in bowl, using electric mixer at high speed. Beat in egg yolks, one at a time, beating well after each addition. Beat in cooled chocolate.

Beat egg whites in another bowl until stiff peaks form, using electric mixer at high speed. Gradually beat in remaining ¼ c. sugar. Beat until stiff, glossy peaks form.

Fold chocolate mixture into egg whites. Then fold in whipped cream. Pour mixture into Chocolate Graham Crust, reserving one fourth of mixture for decorating. Chill until filling sets slightly. With tapered spoon, drop reserved mixture in mounds over top of pie. Cover and chill overnight. Makes 6 to 8 servings.

Chocolate Graham Crust: Combine 1½ c. graham cracker crumbs, ¼ c. brown sugar, packed, ⅛ tsp. ground nutmeg, ⅓ c. melted butter or regular margarine and 1 (1 oz.) square unsweetened chocolate, melted and cooled. Mix thoroughly. Press mixture into 9" pie plate. Chill until firm.

CHOCOLATE NUT TOFFEE PIE

"This tastes like thick cold fudge sauce in a crust," volunteered a Farm Journal editor. She copied the recipe immediately and served it to guests the next evening.

1¼ c. sugar	2 eggs
⅓ c. baking cocoa	1 c. chopped walnuts
2 tblsp. flour	1 (9") unbaked pie shell
½ tsp. salt	Toffee (recipe follows)
½ c. light corn syrup	1 c. heavy cream, whipped
1 (5⅓ oz.) can evaporated milk	

Combine sugar, cocoa, flour and salt in large bowl. Add syrup and evaporated milk. Add eggs, one at a time, beating well after each addition. Stir in walnuts. Turn into pie shell.

151

Bake in 350° oven 55 minutes or until center is set. Cool on rack.

Prepare Toffee. Spread whipped cream over top of pie. Sprinkle with Toffee pieces. Makes 6 to 8 servings.

Toffee: Combine ½ c. sugar, 1 tblsp. light corn syrup, 2 tblsp. evaporated milk, 2 tblsp. butter or regular margarine and ⅛ tsp. salt in 1-qt. heavy saucepan. Cook over low heat, stirring frequently, until mixture is deep amber in color and registers 280° on candy thermometer. Pour mixture into well-buttered 8" square baking pan. Cool completely. Crush candy into small pieces, using rolling pin.

DOUBLE FUDGE BROWNIE PIE

Tastes like a super-rich, super fudgy brownie in a crust. Delicious plain, but utterly divine topped with coffee ice cream and chocolate sauce! A big favorite in our Countryside Test Kitchens.

½ c. butter or regular margarine	1 tsp. vanilla ⅓ c. flour
4 (1 oz.) squares unsweetened chocolate	¼ tsp. salt ¾ c. coarsely chopped
¾ c. brown sugar, packed	walnuts
¼ c. water	1 (9") unbaked pie shell
2 eggs, separated	12 walnut halves

Melt together butter and chocolate in small saucepan over low heat. Remove from heat; cool slightly.

Add brown sugar, water, egg yolks and vanilla; beat well. Stir in flour and salt. Set aside.

Beat egg whites until stiff peaks form, using electric mixer at high speed. Fold egg whites into chocolate mixture. Then fold in chopped walnuts. Pour into pie shell. Arrange walnut halves around edge of pie.

Bake in 350° oven 40 minutes or until set around edges. Cool on rack. Makes 6 to 8 servings.

CHOCOLATE CHERRY PIE

A Colorado ranch wife combined her husband's two favorite ingredients, chocolate and cherries, and perfected this unusual streusel-topped pie.

1 c. sugar	¼ tsp. almond flavoring
¼ c. baking cocoa	1 (9") unbaked pie shell
¼ c. flour	¼ c. flour
Dash of salt	¼ c. sugar
1 (1 lb.) can pitted	3 tblsp. butter or
red sour cherries	regular margarine
1 egg	
2 tblsp. melted butter or	
regular margarine	

Combine 1 c. sugar, cocoa, ¼ c. flour, salt and undrained cherries in large bowl. Add egg, 2 tblsp. melted butter and almond flavoring. Mix well with spoon until blended. Pour into pie shell.

Combine ¼ c. flour and ¼ c. sugar in bowl. Cut in 3 tblsp. butter until mixture is crumbly, using pastry blender or two knives. Sprinkle over pie filling.

Bake in 400° oven 40 minutes or until crust is golden brown. Cool on rack. Makes 6 to 8 servings.

CARIBBEAN FUDGE PIE

A pie that comes from the oven high and puffy. As it cools, it falls, creating a creamy, fudgy center with a brownie-like crust. "Wow—what a great pie," one of our men editors said as he ate the very last fudgy crumb.

¼ c. butter or regular margarine	2 tsp. instant coffee powder
¾ c. brown sugar, packed	1 tsp. rum extract
3 eggs	¼ c. flour
1 (12 oz.) pkg. semisweet chocolate pieces, melted and cooled	1 c. chopped walnuts
	1 (9") unbaked pie shell
	Walnut halves

Cream together butter and brown sugar in bowl until light and fluffy, using electric mixer at medium speed. Add eggs, one at a time, beating well after each addition.

Add cooled chocolate, coffee powder and rum extract, blending well. Stir in flour and chopped walnuts. Turn mixture into pie shell. Arrange walnut halves in circle around edge of pie.

Bake in 375° oven 25 minutes or until set around edges. Cool on rack. Makes 6 to 8 servings.

GERMAN CHOCOLATE PIE

"I am enclosing my family's choice pie," wrote a North Carolina farm woman. "The recipe makes two very rich and delicious pies and it's so simple to make. I serve one to my family and give the second as a 'thank you' to a helpful friend."

3 c. sugar
Dash of salt
7 tblsp. baking cocoa
1 (13½ oz.) can
   evaporated milk
1 tsp. vanilla

4 eggs, beaten
½ c. melted butter or
   regular margarine
2 c. flaked coconut
1 c. chopped pecans
2 (9") unbaked pie shells

Combine sugar, salt and cocoa in bowl. Stir in evaporated milk, vanilla, eggs and melted butter; blend well. Stir in coconut and pecans. Turn mixture into pie shells.

Bake in 350° oven 40 minutes or until set around edge of pies. Cool on racks. Makes 2 pies, 6 to 8 servings each.

FROZEN PEPPERMINT CHOCOLATE PIE

An Illinois farm wife chose this pie as her favorite chocolate recipe because the entire family loves chocolate and she can make it ahead for company or a special occasion. Tastes like a combination of a fudgy mousse and ice cream.

⅔ c. butter or
   regular margarine
1 c. sugar
3 eggs
2 (1 oz.) squares
   unsweetened chocolate,
   melted and cooled

½ c. semisweet choco-
   late pieces, melted
   and cooled
1 (9") graham cracker crust
1 c. heavy cream, whipped
¼ c. crushed peppermint
   stick candy

Cream together butter and sugar in bowl until light and fluffy, using electric mixer at medium speed. Add eggs, one at a time, beating well after each addition. Blend in both chocolates. Turn into graham cracker crust.

Spread with whipped cream. Sprinkle with peppermint candy. Cover and freeze several hours or overnight.

Let stand at room temperature 10 minutes before cutting. Makes 6 to 8 servings.

FROZEN CHOCOLATE CREAM PIE

Tastes like a creamy chocolate ice cream. You can whip up this filling in less than 8 minutes. The Alabama homemaker who shared this recipe with us hoped we would enjoy this fast-fix pie as much as her family does—we do and think you will, too!

2 c. heavy cream
½ tsp. vanilla
1 c. chocolate-flavored
   syrup

1 (9") baked pie shell
¼ c. chopped pecans

Beat together heavy cream and vanilla in bowl until stiff peaks form, using electric mixer at high speed. Carefully fold in chocolate-flavored syrup, ¼ c. at a time. Turn mixture into pie shell. Decorate with chopped pecans. Freeze until firm. Wrap securely in aluminum foil. Continue freezing 8 hours or overnight.

Remove pie from freezer 10 minutes before serving. Makes 6 to 8 servings.

Downright Delicious Desserts & Sauces

Glorious desserts—that's what you'll find in this chapter.

If you have a family who always wants to know, "What are we having for dessert?" We present lots of good old-fashioned homey desserts that will satisfy anyone's sweet tooth.

There are two chocolate bread puddings that we think are just heavenly—not like the ones that are put together just to make use of leftover bread. No, our puddings are the lovely custard type with lots of chocolate. The Layered Chocolate Bread Pudding bakes into three layers: bread, custard and a delicate sponge.

Having company? Please your guests with an elegant Chocolate Charlotte Russe or Chocolate Torte Royale. The torte is a cinnamon-flavored meringue filled with chocolate whipped cream.

Planning a big party? Turn to the recipes for frozen ice cream desserts. Chocolate Almond Swirl serves 20—perfect for a hot summer night.

The last section contains all kinds of fudge sauces. Take your choice of a thin sauce, extra thick or extra chewy. All taste marvelous when poured over ice cream or pound cake.

POMPADOUR PUDDING

Looking for a different dessert? Then do try this. It's a thin vanilla custard topped with a chocolate meringue. And it's good for you, too—a lovely dessert to tempt an invalid's appetite.

1 qt. milk	1 tsp. vanilla
⅔ c. sugar	7 tblsp. sugar
¼ c. flour	2 (1 oz.) squares
¼ tsp. salt	unsweetened chocolate,
4 eggs, separated	melted and cooled
1 tblsp. sugar	

Scald 3 c. of the milk in 3-qt. saucepan.

Combine ⅔ c. sugar, flour and salt in small bowl. Stir in remaining 1 c. milk. Stir mixture into scalded milk. Cook over medium heat, stirring constantly, until mixture starts to boil. (Mixture will be thin.)

Beat egg yolks and 1 tblsp. sugar with fork. Stir some of hot custard into egg yolks. Then stir egg yolk mixture back into hot custard. Cook over low heat, stirring constantly, 2 minutes. Remove from heat. Stir in vanilla. Pour through strainer. Pour mixture into 8 (6 oz.) custard cups.

Beat egg whites in bowl until foamy, using electric mixer at high speed. Gradually add 7 tblsp. sugar, 1 tblsp. at a time, beating until stiff peaks form. Fold in chocolate. Spread meringue mixture over top of each custard cup. Place custard cups on baking sheet.

Bake in 350° oven 5 minutes. Remove from oven and cool at room temperature 20 minutes. Refrigerate until thoroughly chilled, about 3 hours. Makes 8 servings.

CHOCOLATE BREAD PUDDING

If you like plain bread pudding, you will love this rich velvet chocolate one! A nutritious dessert with protein-rich eggs and milk—a superb old-fashioned dessert. A "comforting" food, one of our testers commented.

1¼ c. soft bread crumbs
1 (6 oz.) pkg. semisweet
   chocolate pieces
¼ c. sugar
1½ c. milk
¼ tsp. salt

2 eggs, separated
½ c. milk
2 tblsp. butter or
   regular margarine
½ tsp. vanilla
¼ c. sugar

Combine bread crumbs, ⅔ c. of the chocolate pieces, ¼ c. sugar, 1½ c. milk and salt in top of double boiler. Cook over hot water until chocolate melts, about 5 minutes.

Beat together egg yolks and ½ c. milk in small bowl. Add small amount of chocolate mixture to egg yolks; blend well. Add egg yolk mixture to chocolate mixture; mix well. Stir in butter and vanilla. Pour mixture into 10x6x2" glass baking dish (1½-qt.).

Bake in 350° oven 25 minutes.

While pudding is baking, beat egg whites in bowl until foamy, using electric mixer at high speed. Gradually add ¼ c. sugar, beating until stiff peaks form. Fold in remaining chocolate pieces. Spread meringue over hot pudding. Return to oven and bake 10 more minutes or until meringue is golden brown. Serve warm. Makes 6 servings.

STEAMED CHOCOLATE PUDDING

Most steamed puddings tend to be heavy. Not this one—it's mild flavored and feathery light. An Iowa farmer requests this pudding every year on his birthday. "I hope you like this as much as my husband does," his wife wrote us when she sent in the recipe.

2 c. sifted flour	**4 (1 oz.) squares**
3 tsp. baking powder	**unsweetened chocolate,**
1 c. sugar	**melted and cooled**
2 tblsp. butter or	**1 tsp. vanilla**
regular margarine	**Hard Sauce (recipe**
2 eggs	**follows)**
1 c. milk	

Sift together flour and baking powder; set aside.

Cream together sugar and butter until light and fluffy, using

160

electric mixer at medium speed. Add eggs; beat 1 minute.

Add dry ingredients alternately with milk to creamed mixture, beating well after each addition. Blend in cooled chocolate and vanilla. Spread mixture in well-greased 6½-c. ring mold. Cover tightly with aluminum foil; tie with string.

Place mold on rack in a kettle. Add boiling water to the depth of 1". Cover and steam 1 hour or until toothpick inserted in center of pudding comes out clean. Invert mold onto plate. Serve warm with Hard Sauce. Makes 10 servings.

Hard Sauce: Beat together 2 c. sifted confectioners sugar, ½ c. soft butter or regular margarine and 1 tblsp. vanilla in bowl until smooth and fluffy, using electric mixer at medium speed.

HOT FUDGE PUDDING CAKE

A New York farm woman introduced herself as a very loyal chocolate fan when she sent in this recipe. She found the recipe in a very old cookbook purchased at an auction. "It's a fantastic dessert," she wrote. "Fattening—but worth the splurge!"

1 c. sifted flour	1 tsp. vanilla
¾ c. sugar	¼ c. baking cocoa
3 tblsp. baking cocoa	1 c. light brown
2 tsp. baking powder	sugar, packed
½ tsp. salt	½ c. chopped walnuts
½ c. milk	1¾ c. hot water
2 tblsp. cooking oil	

Sift together flour, sugar, 3 tblsp. cocoa, baking powder and salt into mixing bowl. Add milk, oil and vanilla; blend 1 minute, using

161

electric mixer at medium speed. Pour mixture into greased 9"
square baking pan.

Combine ¼ c. cocoa and brown sugar. Sprinkle over batter.
Then sprinkle with walnuts. Pour hot water over all.

Bake in 350° oven 45 minutes or until toothpick inserted in
cake part comes out clean. Serve warm. Makes 9 servings.

HOT COCOA SOUFFLE

*Because of its feather-light texture and rich chocolate flavor, this is
a Minnesota family's favorite souffle. The golden foamy sauce adds
a special touch.*

6 tblsp. flour	**1½ c. milk**
¾ c. sugar	**5 eggs, separated**
½ c. baking cocoa	**1½ tsp. vanilla**
¼ tsp. salt	**Foamy Sauce (recipe**
6 tblsp. butter or	**follows)**
regular margarine	

Butter and sugar a 1½-qt. souffle dish. Make a collar, by folding aluminum foil into four thicknesses, 3" wide and long enough
to go around souffle dish with a generous overlap. Attach to dish
with masking tape , leaving 2" collar above rim of dish.

Combine flour, sugar, cocoa and salt; set aside.

Melt butter in 2-qt. saucepan. Blend in flour mixture; stir until
smooth. Gradually stir in milk. Cook over medium heat, stirring
constantly, until thick and smooth. Remove from heat.

Beat egg yolks in bowl until thick and lemon-colored, using
electric mixer at high speed. Slowly beat cocoa mixture into egg
yolks, blending well. Add vanilla.

Beat egg whites in another bowl until soft peaks form, using electric mixer at high speed. Fold in cocoa-egg yolk mixture. Pour into prepared dish.

Bake in 350° oven 55 minutes or until knife inserted halfway between center and edge comes out clean. Remove collar. Serve warm with Foamy Sauce. Makes 8 servings.

Foamy Sauce: Melt ¼ c. butter or regular margarine in top of double boiler over boiling water. Stir in 1 c. sifted confectioners sugar; blend until smooth. Beat in 1 egg yolk and cook over simmering water, stirring constantly, 1 minute. Remove from heat; cool slightly. Beat 1 egg white until stiff peaks form, using electric mixer at high speed. Fold egg white into butter mixture. Stir in 1 tsp. vanilla. Serve warm.

LAYERED CHOCOLATE BREAD PUDDING

An excellent bread pudding that looks and tastes a bit different. As it bakes, the pudding separates into three layers: a bread layer, creamy custard layer and a sponge layer. It's an heirloom recipe handed down to a Texas woman from her Pennsylvania Dutch great grandmother.

1 qt. milk	**2 eggs, beaten**
1 c. sugar	**2 c. fresh bread**
½ c. baking cocoa	**crumbs**

Scald milk in saucepan. Remove from heat.

Combine sugar and cocoa in bowl. Add eggs and bread crumbs; mix well. Slowly add scalded milk, blending well. Pour mixture into greased 2-qt. casserole. Set casserole in large baking pan. Add enough boiling water to fill to 1" depth.

Bake in 325° oven 1 hour 20 minutes or until softly set. Serve warm. Makes 6 to 8 servings.

COLD CHOCOLATE SOUFFLE

"Heavenly!" "Marvelous!" "Best souffle I've ever tasted!" These were just a few of the exclamations from our testers when they sampled the first spoonful of this rich, delicate, quivery souffle. They all requested the recipe immediately.

2 envs. unflavored
   gelatin
2 c. milk
1 c. sugar
¼ tsp. salt
4 eggs, separated
1 (12 oz.) pkg. semisweet
   chocolate pieces

1 tsp. vanilla
2 c. heavy cream,
   whipped
Sweetened whipped cream
Chocolate curls

Make a collar for 1 ½ -qt. souffle dish by folding aluminum foil into four thicknesses, 3" wide and long enough to go around the souffle dish with a generous overlap. Attach to dish with masking tape, leaving 3" collar above rim of dish.

Soften gelatin in milk in 2-qt. saucepan 5 minutes.

Combine ½ c. of the sugar, salt and egg yolks in small bowl; blend until smooth. Stir into milk mixture. Add chocolate pieces. Cook over low heat, stirring constantly, until gelatin is dissolved and chocolate is melted, about 8 minutes. Remove from heat. Beat with rotary beater until mixture is smooth. Stir in vanilla. Refrigerate until mixture mounds slightly when dropped from a spoon.

Beat egg whites in bowl until foamy, using electric mixer at high speed. Gradually add remaining ½ c. sugar, beating until very stiff peaks form. Fold egg whites into chocolate mixture. Then fold in whipped cream. Turn mixture into prepared 1½-qt. souffle dish. Refrigerate 2 hours or until set. Remove collar. Decorate with puffs of sweetened whipped cream and chocolate curls. Makes 10 servings.

CHOCOLATE-FILLED CREAM PUFFS

"I consider this cream puff recipe one of my best friends," an Iowa woman wrote us. "I have taken these delicious puffs to bake sales, covered dish dinners and silent auctions, and they are my favorite food to give to a friend who is extra busy. I sometimes exchange a batch of my cream puffs for one of my neighbor's fabulous chocolate pies."

1 c. sifted flour	4 eggs
¼ tsp. salt	Chocolate Filling
½ c. butter or	(recipe follows)
regular margarine	Chocolate Glaze
1 c. boiling water	(recipe follows)

Sift together flour and salt; set aside.

Combine butter and boiling water in 2-qt. saucepan. Cook over low heat until butter melts. Add flour mixture all at once. Stir vigorously over low heat until mixture forms a ball and leaves the sides of the saucepan. Remove from heat.

Add eggs, one at a time, beating thoroughly after each addition. Continue beating until mixture is glossy. Drop by tablespoonfuls, about 2" apart, on greased baking sheets.

165

Bake in 425° oven 30 minutes or until golden brown. (Do not peek during baking.) Remove from baking sheets; cool on racks. When cool, remove top with knife. Fill with Chocolate Filling, using 2 tblsp. for each. Replace top. Drizzle with Chocolate Glaze, using 1 tblsp. for each. Makes 24.

Chocolate Filling: Prepare 1 (3⅝ oz.) pkg. chocolate pudding and pie filling with 1½ c. milk according to package directions for pudding. Cool well. Fold in 1 c. heavy cream, whipped.

Chocolate Glaze: Combine 1 c. sifted confectioners sugar, 2 (1 oz.) squares unsweetened chocolate, melted and cooled, 2 tblsp. soft butter or regular margarine, dash of salt, ¼ tsp. vanilla and 2 tblsp. boiling water in bowl. Blend until smooth.

CHOCOLATE CREAM JELLY

A real old-fashioned recipe. Very different and delicious, it is a light dessert to serve after a huge company dinner. Top with whipped cream or a drizzle of chocolate sauce.

1 tblsp. unflavored gelatin	½ c. sugar
1 c. cold milk	1 c. heavy cream
1 (1 oz.) square unsweetened chocolate, cut up	½ tsp. vanilla
	Sweetened whipped cream

Soften gelatin in ¼ c. of the milk 5 minutes.

Combine chocolate and remaining ¾ c. milk in top of double boiler. Cook over hot water until chocolate is melted. Remove from heat. Beat until smooth with rotary beater.

Stir in sugar and softened gelatin. Refrigerate until mixture is like a thick syrup.

Whip heavy cream and vanilla in bowl until stiff peaks form, using electric mixer at high speed. Fold chocolate mixture into whipped cream. Pour into lightly oiled 3½-c. mold or 6 individual molds. Refrigerate until set, about 3 hours.

Remove from mold(s). Decorate with puffs of sweetened whipped cream. Makes 6 servings.

CHOCOLATE TORTE ROYALE

An elegant European-style dessert. The crackly-crisp cinnamon meringue shell is filled with a thin layer of rich chocolate and topped with chocolate whipped cream. A chocolate lover's delight. (See photo, Plate 4.)

Meringue Shell (recipe follows)	**2 egg yolks**
	¼ c. water
1 (6 oz.) pkg. semisweet chocolate pieces	**1 c. heavy cream**
	¼ tsp. ground cinnamon

Prepare Meringue Shell.

Place chocolate pieces in top of double boiler. Melt over hot water. Remove from heat. Spread 2 tblsp. of the melted chocolate in bottom of cooled Meringue Shell.

Beat together egg yolks and water in small bowl. Add egg yolk mixture all at once to melted chocolate. Beat together until mixture is smooth, using wire whisk or rotary beater. Place over simmering water. Cook 2 minutes, stirring constantly, until mixture is slightly thickened. Remove from heat. Cool to room temperature.

Whip cream and cinnamon in another bowl until stiff peaks

167

form, using electric mixer at high speed. Fold cooled chocolate mixture into whipped cream. Turn into Meringue Shell. Cover and refrigerate until set, about 4 hours. Makes 6 to 8 servings.

Meringue Shell: Draw an 8" circle on heavy brown paper. Place on baking sheet. Combine 2 egg whites, ⅛ tsp. salt and ½ tsp. vinegar in bowl. Beat with electric mixer at high speed until foamy. Combine ½ c. sugar and ¼ tsp. cinnamon. Gradually add sugar mixture to egg whites, beating until very stiff glossy peaks form. Spread meringue in 8" circle, building up 1½" rim around edge of circle. If you wish to use a decorating tube, spread 1 c. meringue in 8" circle. Place remaining meringue in decorating tube with extra large star tip, about ¾" wide. Make a shell border on edge of circle, 1¼" high. (Complete shell is about 9½" wide.)

Bake in 275° oven 1 hour. Turn off heat, but leave shell in oven 2 more hours with door closed. Carefully remove paper from meringue shell. Place on serving plate.

PEPPERMINT CHOCOLATE MOUSSE

Especially designed for the busy hostess. In less than 10 minutes, you can create this fancy mousse. A creamy light dessert with a very subtle peppermint flavor.

1 (6 oz.) pkg. semisweet chocolate pieces	**4 eggs, separated**
	¼ tsp. peppermint extract
5 tblsp. very hot coffee	

Combine chocolate pieces and coffee in blender jar. Cover and blend at high speed until smooth. Add egg yolks and blend at high speed until thick and smooth.

Beat egg whites in bowl until stiff peaks form, using electric mixer at high speed. Beat a small amount of whites into chocolate. Then fold remaining chocolate mixture into egg whites with peppermint extract. Pour into serving bowl or parfait glasses. Refrigerate at least 1 hour or until set. Serve topped with sweetened whipped cream if you wish. Makes 6 (½ cup) servings.

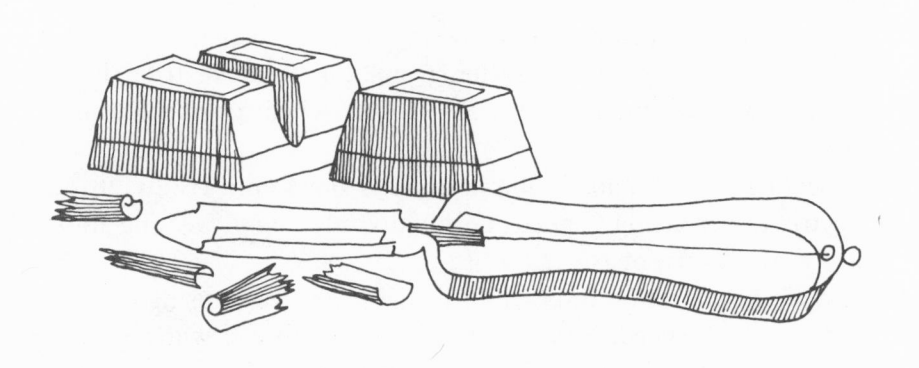

CHOCOLATE CHARLOTTE RUSSE

A chocolate whipped cream dessert surrounded by golden ladyfingers. A luscious, light ending to a festive meal. (See photo, Plate 8.)

20 ladyfingers, split	**⅓ c. water**
1 env. unflavored gelatin	**2 eggs, separated**
¼ c. water	**1 tsp. vanilla**
1 (6 oz.) pkg. semisweet chocolate pieces	**½ c. sugar**
	2 c. heavy cream

Line the sides of 8" springform pan with ladyfingers (curved side toward the outside edge). To line bottom of pan, cut a diagonal slice off each side of one end of each remaining ladyfinger to form wedges. Arrange in bottom of pan, curved side down with pointed ends in center. Cut a small round from remaining ladyfinger to fit in the center. Cover with plastic wrap and set aside.

Soften gelatin in ¼ c. water 5 minutes.

Melt chocolate pieces in top of double boiler over simmering water. Beat together ⅓ c. water and egg yolks. Add egg yolk mixture all at once to melted chocolate. Beat until smooth, using wire whisk or rotary beater. Cook over simmering water 2 minutes, stirring constantly. Stir in softened gelatin. Remove from heat. Refrigerate until mixture mounds slightly when dropped from a spoon.

Beat egg whites and vanilla in another bowl until foamy, using electric mixer at high speed. Gradually add sugar, beating until stiff peaks form. Set aside.

Whip heavy cream in bowl until stiff peaks form, using electric mixer at high speed. Fold whipped cream into egg whites. Then fold in chocolate mixture. Pour mixture into ladyfinger-lined pan. Cover and refrigerate 4 hours or until set. Makes 12 servings.

FROZEN FUDGE POPS

"Youngsters prefer these frozen chocolate pops to the commercial type, and they are more nourishing, too," wrote A North Dakota woman. A great treat for a hot summer day—all of our adult testers liked these creamy frozen treats.

1 (4 oz.) pkg. chocolate	**¼ c. sugar**
pudding and pie filling	**3½ c. milk**

Combine all ingredients in saucepan. Cook over medium heat, stirring constantly, until mixture comes to a boil. Remove from heat. Mixture is very thin. Pour into Popsicle forms. Freeze fudge pops until firm. Makes 14 (3½ oz.) pops.

BANANA SPLIT DESSERT

A festive summer dessert submitted by an Iowa farm woman. Her family's three favorite foods are chocolate, ice cream and bananas. This yummy dessert combines all three. Good to make when you're expecting a crowd—it serves 20 people.

24 chocolate sandwich cookies, crushed	**½ c. butter or regular margarine**
¼ c. melted butter or regular margarine	**1 (6 oz.) pkg. semisweet chocolate pieces**
3 bananas	**1½ c. evaporated milk**
½ gal. mint chip flavor ice cream, softened	**2 c. sifted confectioners sugar**
½ c. toasted chopped walnuts	**1 tsp. vanilla**

Combine cookie crumbs and ¼ c. butter in bowl; mix well. Press mixture into 13x9x2" baking pan. Slice bananas; arrange over crust in even layer.

Spread softened ice cream over bananas. Sprinkle with walnuts. Freeze until firm.

Combine ½ c. butter, chocolate pieces, evaporated milk and confectioners sugar in saucepan; mix well. Cook over medium heat, stirring constantly, until mixture just starts to boil. Remove from heat. Stir in vanilla. Cool well.

Pour chocolate mixture evenly over all. Cover with aluminum foil and store in freezer. Remove from freezer 10 minutes before cutting. Cut in squares. Makes 20 servings.

BROWNIE TWIRL BAKED ALASKA

A show-stopper dessert! Slice it down and discover a chewy brownie layer, topped with creamy ice cream and blanketed with a soft brown sugar meringue. "Wow—this is fantastic," sighed one of our testers, who had temporarily abandoned her diet to sample this dessert.

2 (1 oz.) squares
    unsweetened chocolate
½ c. butter or
    regular margarine
2 eggs
1 c. sugar
1 tsp. vanilla
¾ c. sifted flour
½ tsp. baking powder
¼ tsp. salt

½ c. chopped walnuts
1 qt. block fudge ripple ice
    cream
4 egg whites
¼ tsp. cream of tartar
½ c. brown sugar, packed
½ (1 oz.) square
    unsweetened chocolate,
    melted and cooled

Melt together 2 oz. chocolate and butter in saucepan over low heat. Cool well.

Combine eggs, sugar, vanilla and cooled chocolate in mixing bowl. Beat with electric mixer at medium speed until blended.

Sift together flour, baking powder and salt. Stir into chocolate mixture with walnuts. Pour chocolate mixture. into greased 9" square baking pan.

Bake in 350° oven 30 minutes or until done. Cool in pan 10 minutes. Remove from pan; cool on rack.

Measure block of ice cream. Trim brownie layer so it is ½" larger on all sides than ice cream block. Place brownie layer on aluminum foil-covered wooden board. Center ice cream on brownie layer. Place in freezer while preparing egg whites.

Beat egg whites and cream of tartar in bowl until foamy, using electric mixer at high speed. Gradually add brown sugar, beating until stiff, glossy peaks form.

Spread meringue over entire surface of ice cream and brownie layer, right down to aluminum foil. Meringue should be at least 1" thick.

Bake in 500° oven 3 minutes or until lightly browned. Drizzle with ½ oz. cooled chocolate. Makes 10 servings.

NEAPOLITAN DESSERT

"Outrageously delicious," was the unanimous vote from our test kitchens when we tried this frozen dessert. It tastes like a banana split, only much better.

¼ lb. graham crackers
¼ c. sugar
¼ c. melted butter or
  regular margarine
3 medium bananas
½ gal. Neapolitan flavor
  ice cream
1 c. chopped walnuts
1 (6 oz.) pkg. semisweet
  chocolate pieces

½ c. butter or
  regular margarine
2 c. sifted confectioners
  sugar
1½ c. evaporated milk
1 tsp. vanilla
2 c. heavy cream
¼ c. sugar
2 tsp. vanilla

Crush graham crackers to form crumbs. Combine graham cracker crumbs, ¼ c. sugar and ¼ c. butter in bowl; mix until blended. Reserve ½ c. crumbs. Press remaining crumbs in bottom of 15½x10½x1" jelly roll pan.

Slice bananas; arrange in a single layer over crust. Cut block of ice cream into ½" slices; place over bananas, making an even layer. Sprinkle with chopped walnuts. Freeze until firm.

Melt chocolate pieces and ½ c. butter in saucepan over low heat. Add confectioners sugar and evaporated milk; blend well. Cook over medium heat, stirring constantly, until mixture thickens. Remove from heat. Stir in 1 tsp. vanilla. Cool well.

Spread chocolate sauce over ice cream layer. Freeze until firm.

Whip heavy cream in bowl until it begins to thicken, using electric mixer at high speed. Gradually add ¼ c. sugar and 2 tsp. vanilla. Beat until soft peaks form. Spread over chocolate layer.

Sprinkle with reserved ½ c. crumbs. Cover with aluminum foil. Store in freezer. Remove from freezer 10 minutes before serving. Cut into 3½ x 2" pieces. Makes 24 servings.

CHOCOLATE ALMOND SWIRL

"A recipe that is excellent to make and serve to a large group but it can easily be cut in half," wrote an Iowa farm wife. We think it's a super dessert to serve on a hot summer night when friends drop in to visit.

5 (1 oz.) almond milk chocolate candy bars	**½ c. toasted whole almonds**
½ c. butter or regular margarine	**3 egg whites, stiffly beaten**
3 egg yolks, beaten	**½ c. vanilla wafer crumbs**
½ c. sifted confectioners sugar	**½ gal. vanilla ice cream**

Melt together candy bars and butter in saucepan over low heat. Stir some of chocolate mixture into egg yolks; blend well. Stir egg yolk mixture into chocolate. Cook over low heat several minutes. Remove from heat. Stir in confectioners sugar and almonds. Cool well at room temperature.

Fold egg whites into chocolate mixture. Line 13x9x2" baking pan with vanilla wafer crumbs.

Soften ice cream and spoon into crumb-lined baking pan. Ripple chocolate mixture through ice cream. Freeze until hard. Let stand 5 minutes before serving. Makes 20 servings.

CHOCOLATE PEPPERMINT FROZEN DESSERT

"I have given this recipe to only three people—my two daughters-in-law and my best friend. However, now I'd like to share it with you," wrote a North Dakota farm woman. "Don't try to crush the hard candies in your grinder," she warned. "Use a hammer or rolling pin." (See photo, Plate 5.)

**2 c. vanilla wafer
crumbs
¼ c. melted butter
or regular margarine
1½ c. sifted confectioners
sugar
½ c. butter or
regular margarine
3 eggs
2 (1 oz.) squares
unsweetened chocolate,
melted and cooled**

**1½ c. heavy cream
3 c. miniature marshmallows
¼ c. crushed peppermint
candy
½ (1 oz.) square
unsweetened chocolate,
melted and cooled**

Mix together vanilla wafer crumbs and ¼ c. butter in bowl; press mixture into 13x9x2" baking pan. Refrigerate while preparing filling.

175

Cream together confectioners sugar and ½ c. butter in bowl until light and fluffy, using electric mixer at high speed. Add eggs, one at a time, beating well after each addition. Blend in 2 oz. cooled chocolate. Spread mixture evenly over crumb crust. Refrigerate while preparing topping.

Whip heavy cream in bowl until stiff peaks form. Fold in marshmallows. Spread over chocolate layer. Sprinkle with peppermint candy. Freeze until firm, about 3 hours.

Before serving, drizzle with ½ oz. cooled chocolate. Makes 16 servings.

CHOCOLATE RUM TORTONI

A party dessert that a North Carolina farm wife always serves for very special occasions. This super-quick, elegant recipe will delight your guests.

1 egg, separated
½ c. sifted confectioners
  sugar
¼ tsp. rum flavoring
1 c. heavy cream,
  whipped

⅛ tsp. salt
1 (1 oz.) square
  unsweetened chocolate,
  grated
½ c. chopped pecans

Blend together egg yolk, confectioners sugar and rum flavoring. Fold into whipped cream.

Beat egg white with salt in bowl until stiff peaks form, using electric mixer at high speed. Fold into cream mixture. Fold in chocolate. Reserve 2 tblsp. of pecans. Fold in remaining pecans.

Spoon mixture into 2½" paper-lined muffin pan cups. Sprinkle with reserved 2 tblsp. pecans. Freeze until firm. Serve in paper cups. Makes 8 servings.

MILK CHOCOLATE PUDDING

"This is my husband's favorite pudding," wrote a Missouri woman. "It was handed down through his family and makes a nice thick pudding. Sometimes I pour it into a baked pie shell and top with whipped cream," she said.

1⅓ c. sugar	4 c. milk, scalded
⅔ c. flour	1 egg, beaten
4 tblsp. baking cocoa	2 tsp. vanilla
Pinch of salt	

Combine sugar, flour, cocoa and salt in saucepan. Gradually stir in scalded milk and egg; blend well. Cook over medium heat, stirring constantly, until mixture thickens. Remove from heat; stir in vanilla. Spoon mixture into 6 dessert dishes. Refrigerate several hours or until set. Makes 6 servings.

DARK CHOCOLATE PUDDING

A pudding for chocolate fans who prefer a rich-bodied flavor instead of the milder milk chocolate. Serve plain or top with a swirl of whipped cream and a walnut half.

½ c. sugar	1 egg, beaten
3 tblsp. flour	½ tsp. vanilla
⅛ tsp. salt	1 tblsp. butter or
1½ c. milk	regular margarine
1 (1 oz.) square	Sweetened whipped cream
unsweetened chocolate,	
cut up	

177

Combine sugar, flour and salt in 2-qt. saucepan; mix well. Gradually stir in milk, blending well. Stir in chocolate and egg. Cook over medium heat, stirring constantly, until mixture thickens. Remove from heat. Stir in vanilla and butter. Spoon into 4 dessert dishes. Refrigerate several hours or until set. Top with sweetened whipped cream. Makes 4 servings.

EASY CHOCOLATE FONDUE

"I especially like this recipe," wrote a North Dakota farm woman, "because now my children will try all kinds of fruit. If there is any left over, I reheat it and serve as an ice cream topping."

1 (6 oz.) pkg. semisweet chocolate pieces	**Assorted fruits, marshmallows, cake pieces, etc., as desired**
½ c. honey	
⅔ c. evaporated milk	

Combine chocolate pieces and honey in small saucepan. Place over low heat until melted; stir until smooth. Gradually stir in evaporated milk, blending well. Pour mixture into fondue pot or small chafing dish and keep warm.

Pass cut-up assorted fresh fruits, marshmallows and pieces of cake for dunking. Makes 1⅔ cups.

FUDGY CHOCOLATE SAUCE

"This is an inexpensive, quick, easy recipe that can be made by older children in the family," wrote a Michigan homemaker. "Actually, it

is a fudge recipe that I cut in half but omit cooking to fudge temper-
ature and use as a sauce over eclairs or pound cake as well as ice
cream." Our testers liked it, too.

⅓ c. baking cocoa   ¾ c. milk
1½ c. sugar   ½ tsp. vanilla
Dash of salt

Combine cocoa, sugar and salt in 2-qt. saucepan. Gradually stir
in milk. Cook over medium heat, stirring constantly, until mixture
comes to a rolling boil. Remove from heat. Stir in vanilla. Serve
warm or cold over ice cream. Makes about 1 cup.

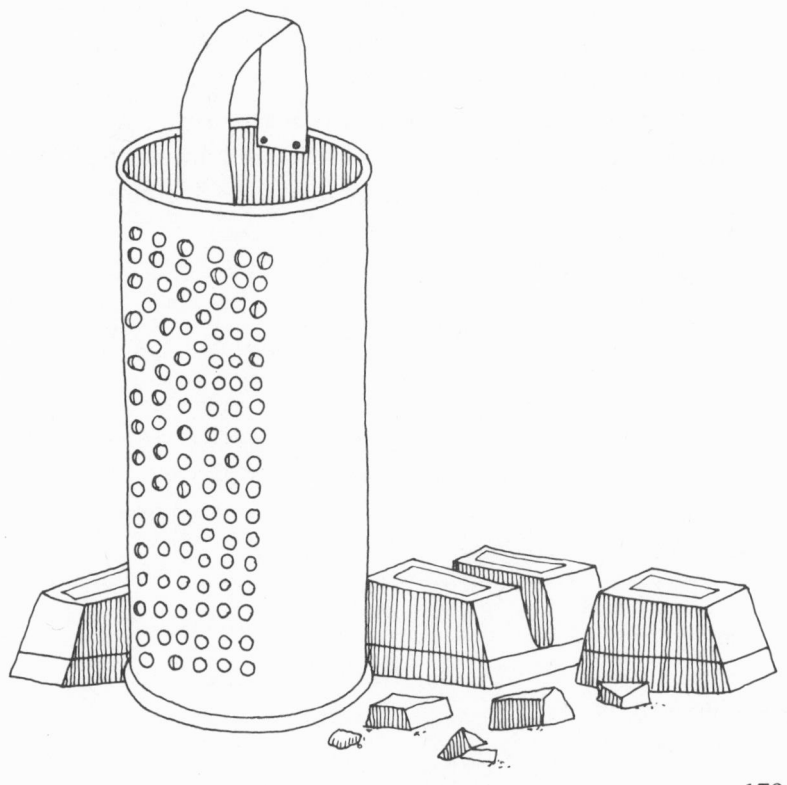

HONEY CHOCOLATE SAUCE

If you have a super sweet tooth, this is the sauce for you. The honey adds extra sweetness and smoothness—it's a lovely thick sauce that clings to ice cream like a chocolate cloak.

¼ c. butter or	½ c. water
regular margarine	6 large marshmallows
1 tblsp. cornstarch	⅛ tsp. salt
3 tblsp. baking cocoa	1 tsp. vanilla
½ c. honey	

Melt butter in 2-qt. heavy saucepan. Stir in cornstarch and cocoa to form a paste. Stir in honey and water. Cook over medium heat, stirring constantly, until mixture thickens and starts to boil. Add marshmallows and salt. Continue cooking just long enough to melt marshmallows. Remove from heat. Stir in vanilla. Serve warm over ice cream. Store leftover sauce in refrigerator. Reheat over low heat. Makes 1¼ cups.

PEANUT BUTTER FUDGE SAUCE

A medium-thick sauce that's chock-full of crunchy peanuts. "Our kids say this is the best chocolate topping for ice cream," said a Pennsylvania farm woman. A yummy combination of two great flavors, and so easy to make, too.

1 c. sugar	½ c. chocolate-
1 c. water	flavored syrup
1 c. crunch-style	
peanut butter	

Combine sugar and water in 2-qt. saucepan. Bring mixture to a boil, over medium heat, stirring constantly. Boil 5 minutes.

Stir in peanut butter and chocolate syrup. Return to medium heat. Bring to a boil, stirring constantly. Cool to lukewarm. Serve over ice cream. Makes 2¼ cups.

CHEWY FUDGE SAUCE

Pour this sauce over ice cream and watch it immediately harden into a chocolate caramel consistency. "Does tend to stick to your teeth, but that doesn't matter," wrote a Minnesota woman. "It is an utterly scrumptious sauce—my family loves it!"

2 (1 oz.) squares unsweetened chocolate, cut up	**⅓ c. boiling water**
	1 c. sugar
	2 tblsp. light corn syrup
1 tblsp. butter or regular margarine	**1 tsp. vanilla**

Combine chocolate and butter in 2-qt. heavy saucepan. Cook over low heat until melted. Add boiling water, stirring well. Stir in sugar and corn syrup. Cook over medium heat, stirring constantly, until mixture comes to a boil. Boil 5 minutes. Remove from heat. Stir in vanilla. Serve warm over ice cream. Leftover sauce can be stored in refrigerator. Reheat over low heat. Makes about 1 cup.

MOM'S CHOCOLATE SAUCE

"My husband's favorite dessert is this homemade syrup poured warm over a piece of chocolate cake," wrote a Wisconsin farm wife. "My

181

favorite dessert," she continued, "is this syrup cold, poured over ice cream, and the kids like to make chocolate milk and hot chocolate with it. You can see this is a well-used recipe in our house."

---

1 (1 oz.) square
    unsweetened chocolate
1 tblsp. butter or
    regular margarine
⅓ c. boiling water

1 c. sugar
2 tblsp. light corn
    syrup
⅛ tsp. salt
1 tsp. vanilla

Melt together chocolate and butter in 2-qt. heavy saucepan over low heat. Gradually stir in boiling water. Continue cooking over medium heat, stirring constantly, until mixture boils. Stir in sugar and corn syrup. Bring to a boil, stirring constantly. Remove from heat. Cool 5 minutes. Stir in salt and vanilla. Serve warm or cold over ice cream. Makes 1 cup.

VERY THICK FUDGE SAUCE

"A sauce so thick that it's almost like a pudding, but that's the way my four children and husband like it," wrote an Ohio farm wife. We liked it, too!

---

1 (12 oz.) pkg. semisweet
    chocolate pieces
1 (13 oz.) can
    evaporated milk

3 tblsp. butter or
    regular margarine

Combine all ingredients in 2-qt. heavy saucepan. Cook over low heat, stirring constantly, until chocolate is melted and mixture is thick and smooth. Serve warm over ice cream or squares of cake.

Leftover sauce can be stored in refrigerator. Reheat over low heat. Makes about 2½ cups.

FUDGE/PECAN TOPPING

A candy bar sauce full of pecans that make it ever so elegant— everyone gets a big helping of nuts in each spoonful. A top choice among the Farm Journal test kitchen and tasting staff.

6 (1½ oz.) Milky
Way candy bars, cut up
6 (1 oz.) squares semi-
sweet chocolate,
cut up

1 c. milk
1⅓ c. small pecan
halves

Combine candy bars, semisweet chocolate and milk in top of double boiler. Place over simmering water. Cook, stirring constantly, until chocolate is melted and mixture is smooth. Stir in pecans. Remove from heat. Serve warm over ice cream or squares of cake. Store leftover sauce in refrigerator. Reheat over low heat. Makes about 3 cups.

HOT FUDGE PEPPERMINT SAUCE

"Rich and delicious," wrote an Ohio woman. Serve hot over ice cream. The mint is just right—tastes like a melted peppermint patty.

1 c. sugar
1 (13 oz.) can
    evaporated milk
4 (1 oz.) squares
    unsweetened chocolate,
    cut up

¼ tsp. salt
¼ c. butter or
    regular margarine
1 tsp. vanilla
¼ tsp. peppermint
    flavoring

Combine sugar and evaporated milk in 2-qt. heavy saucepan. Bring to a rolling boil, stirring constantly, over medium heat. Boil 1 minute, stirring constantly. Add chocolate and salt. Stir until chocolate is melted. Remove from heat. Beat with rotary beater until smooth. Stir in butter, vanilla and peppermint flavoring. Cool to lukewarm. Serve over ice cream. Makes 2⅓ cups.

CHOCOLATE SYRUP SAUCE

This recipe is for folks who like a thin chocolate topping that pools in the bottom of the saucer when it's poured over ice cream.

½ c. baking cocoa
⅓ c. light corn syrup
6 tblsp. water
1½ c. sugar
¼ tsp. salt

1 c. milk
3 tblsp. butter or
    regular margarine
½ tsp. vanilla

Combine cocoa, corn syrup and water in 2-qt. heavy saucepan. Cook over medium heat, stirring constantly, until mixture is well blended. Stir in sugar, salt and milk. Continue cooking, stirring constantly, until temperature reaches 220° on candy thermometer. Remove from heat. Stir in butter and vanilla. Cool to lukewarm. Serve over ice cream. Leftover sauce can be refrigerated. Reheat over low heat. Makes 2⅓ cups.

Fudge and More Fudge

Remember when your mother made fudge while you waited anxiously to scrape the bottom of the pot? Remember the alluring smell of the chocolate mixture bubbling in the pots . . . and how your arm ached as you beat and beat the fudge until it was set?

Today the excitement of making fudge remains, but the methods have been simplified. You can have delicious fudge without all the beating or the complicated "soft-ball stage" testing.

The recipes in this chapter reflect how most of today's farm homemakers feel about fudge making. They like the easy new varieties, such as the no-cook fudge or the fudge that cooks for 10 minutes and is beaten for just a few minutes or not at all. And now, there's super speedy microwave fudge, cooked in just two minutes. Alas, the wonderful aroma is missing, but the microwave fudge is delightful to eat.

This chapter offers a variety of fool-proof fudges to make for gifts or to treat the family. Do you like a mild chocolate flavor? Then make Quick Potato Fudge. But if you prefer devastatingly rich candy, stir up French Fudge. And then go on to try the rest.

185

DOUBLE CHOCOLATE FUDGE

"When I was in college, I used to make this fudge in my popcorn popper. I won a prize with this recipe in a dormitory bake-off," an Illinois woman told us when she sent this two-layer fudge recipe.

2½ c. sugar	¾ c. chopped walnuts
1 c. evaporated milk	1 tsp. vanilla
¼ c. butter or	1 (6 oz.) pkg. semisweet
regular margarine	chocolate pieces
¼ tsp. salt	1 (6 oz.) pkg. milk
1½ c. miniature	chocolate pieces
marshmallows	

Combine sugar, evaporated milk, butter and salt in 2-qt. heavy saucepan. Cook over medium heat, stirring constantly, until mixture comes to a rolling boil. Boil 6 minutes, stirring often. Remove from heat.

Add marshmallows, walnuts and vanilla; stir until well blended. Remove 1½ c. hot mixture and place in bowl. Add semisweet chocolate pieces; stir until well blended and chocolate is melted. Quickly spread chocolate mixture in buttered 8" square baking pan. Add milk chocolate pieces to remaining hot mixture; stir until blended. Spread evenly over top of first layer. Cool until firm. Cut into 1¼" squares. Makes 36 pieces.

CALIFORNIA CREAM FUDGE

Like extra-rich fudge? California Cream Fudge is what a Montana woman calls this recipe, which she has been using for years with

*perfect results every time. She said she never fails to receive requests
for her fudge whenever she gives it as a gift.*

3 c. sugar
1 c. light cream
2 (1 oz.) squares
   unsweetened chocolate
3 tblsp. light corn syrup
¼ tsp. salt

1 tblsp. butter or
   regular margarine
1 tsp. vanilla
1 c. coarsely chopped
   pecans

Combine sugar, light cream, chocolate, corn syrup and salt in
3-qt. heavy saucepan. Cook over medium heat, stirring constantly,
until mixture boils. Continue cooking to soft ball stage (234°) on
candy thermometer; do not stir. Remove from heat.

Add butter; cool to lukewarm (110°) without stirring.

Stir in vanilla and beat with wooden spoon until candy thickens
and loses its gloss. Quickly stir in pecans. Turn mixture into buttered 8" square baking pan. Score while warm. Cool and cut into
1¼" squares. Makes 36 pieces.

MOTHER'S COCOA FUDGE

*A Missouri woman remembers that during World War II, her moth-
er would begin saving sugar early in the summer to make this fudge
at Christmastime.*

4 c. sugar
⅓ c. baking cocoa
¼ tsp. salt
⅛ tsp. cream of tartar
1 (13 oz.) can evaporated
   milk

2 tblsp. butter or
   regular margarine
2 tsp. vanilla

Combine sugar, cocoa, salt and cream of tartar in 3-qt. heavy saucepan. Gradually stir in evaporated milk. Cook over medium heat, stirring constantly, until mixture starts to boil. Continue cooking to soft ball stage (234°) without stirring.

Add butter; cool to lukewarm (110°) without stirring.

Stir in vanilla. Beat until thick enough to knead easily. Knead mixture on waxed paper until smooth. Shape mixture into 2 rolls, 12" long and 1½" in diameter. Cut into ½" thick slices to serve. Makes 48 pieces.

VELVET CHOCOLATE FUDGE

A smooth, glossy, milk chocolate-flavored fudge that's loaded with big chunks of walnuts. "My very favorite candy to make during the Christmas season for a last-minute gift," a Wyoming farm woman told us. This fudge was also popular in our Test Kitchens.

4½ c. sugar
1 tblsp. cornstarch
½ tsp. salt
1 (13 oz.) can evaporated milk
½ c. butter or regular margarine
1 (16 oz.) pkg. regular marshmallows
1 (12 oz.) pkg. semisweet chocolate pieces
1 (8 oz.) milk chocolate candy bar, broken up
2 tsp. vanilla
2 c. chopped walnuts

Combine sugar, cornstarch and salt in 5-qt. heavy Dutch oven. Stir in evaporated milk and butter. Cook over medium heat, stirring constantly, until mixture comes to a rolling boil. Boil 8 minutes, stirring frequently. Remove from heat.

Stir in marshmallows, semisweet chocolate pieces, milk chocolate and vanilla; beat until smooth. Stir in walnuts. Pour into buttered 15½x10½x1" jelly roll pan. Cool and cut into 1¼" squares. Makes 8 dozen pieces.

MARSHMALLOW FUDGE

"A quick, easy, delicious fudge that I know you'll enjoy making and eating," a Missouri woman said when she submitted this recipe. We all agreed, especially the testers who like a deep chocolate flavor.

1⅔ c. sugar	15 large marshmallows
2 tblsp. butter or	1½ c. semisweet chocolate
regular margarine	pieces
⅔ c. evaporated milk	1 tsp. vanilla
Dash of salt	½ c. chopped pecans

Combine sugar, butter, evaporated milk and salt in 2-qt. heavy saucepan. Cook over medium heat, stirring constantly, until mixture comes to a boil. Continue cooking 10 minutes, stirring frequently. Remove from heat.

Stir in marshmallows, chocolate pieces, vanilla and pecans. Stir quickly until marshmallows and chocolate are melted. Pour mixture into buttered 8" square baking pan. Cool well. Cut into 1½" squares. Makes 25 pieces.

CHOCOLATE BUTTERSCOTCH FUDGE

A super-easy fudge to make because the electric mixer does all of the beating. An original recipe from a Georgia homemaker. She com-

bined three different fudge recipes and came up with this fast-fix fudge that doesn't require refrigeration.

1 c. sugar	1 (6 oz.) pkg. butterscotch
1 (15 oz.) can sweetened	flavored pieces
condensed milk (not	¼ c. butter or
evaporated)	regular margarine
½ c. water	1 tsp. vanilla
1 (6 oz.) pkg. semisweet	1 c. chopped walnuts
chocolate pieces	

Combine sugar, sweetened condensed milk, water, chocolate and butterscotch pieces in 3-qt. heavy saucepan. Cook over medium heat, stirring constantly, to soft ball stage (234°). Remove from heat.

Combine butter and vanilla in mixing bowl. Pour hot mixture into bowl. Beat with electric mixer at high speed until mixture starts to thicken. Stir in walnuts. Spread into greased 9" square baking pan. Cool and cut in 1½" squares. Makes 36 pieces.

FRENCH CHOCOLATE FUDGE

Especially for fudge lovers who prefer a less sweet fudge. In fact, it tastes like semisweet chocolate. Cut in tiny pieces and serve as dessert with coffee.

3 (6 oz.) pkgs. semisweet	1½ tsp. vanilla
chocolate pieces	Dash of salt
1 (14 oz.) can sweetened	½ c. chopped walnuts
condensed milk (not	
evaporated)	

Melt chocolate pieces in top of double boiler over hot water. Remove from heat.

Stir in sweetened condensed milk, vanilla, salt and walnuts. Stir until smooth. Turn into buttered 8" square baking pan. Chill until firm. Cut into 1½" squares. Store in refrigerator. Makes 25 pieces.

FAVORITE FAMILY FUDGE

Rich chocolate-flavored fudge with a subtle cherry flavor. "This fudge recipe was handed down from my grandmother to my mother and then to me. We all know this recipe by heart. This is the first time I've ever written it down," wrote a South Dakota farm woman.

3 c. sugar
1 c. evaporated milk
3 (1 oz.) squares
   unsweetened chocolate
3 tblsp. light corn syrup
¼ tsp. salt

3 tblsp. butter or
   regular margarine
3 tsp. vanilla
1 (6 oz.) jar red maraschino
   cherries, well drained
   and chopped (½ c.)

Combine sugar, evaporated milk, chocolate, corn syrup and salt in 3-qt. heavy saucepan. Cook over medium heat, stirring constantly, until mixture boils. Cook to soft ball stage (234°) without stirring. Remove from heat.

Add butter; cool to lukewarm (110°) without stirring.

Stir in vanilla. Beat until fudge stiffens and loses its gloss. Quickly stir in maraschino cherries. Turn mixture into buttered 8" baking pan. Score while warm. Cut into 1¼" squares when cooled. Makes 36 pieces.

CHOCOLATE WONDER FUDGE

"My twelve-year-old son likes to make this fudge as it's so easy and he has a chocolate treat in no time at all," wrote a New York farm woman. For a change, why not substitute chopped peanuts for half of the crunchy cereal?

1 (6 oz.) pkg. semisweet
   chocolate pieces
¼ c. butter or
   regular margarine
¼ c. light corn syrup

1 tsp. vanilla
1 c. sifted confectioners
   sugar
3 c. toasted rice
   cereal

Melt together chocolate pieces and butter in saucepan over low heat. Remove from heat. Stir in corn syrup; blend well. Stir in vanilla and confectioners sugar, blending well. Add toasted rice cereal, mixing lightly until well coated. Spread mixture evenly in buttered 8" square baking pan. Cover and refrigerate until firm. Cut into 2" squares. Makes 16 pieces.

TWO-TONE FUDGE

"Our Christmas wouldn't be complete without a dish of Two-Tone Fudge," wrote a Kansas farm wife. "We think it looks more elegant than regular fudge, yet it's simple to make."

2 c. brown sugar, packed	1 tsp. vanilla
1 c. sugar	1 (6 oz.) pkg. butterscotch
1 c. evaporated milk	flavored pieces
½ c. butter or	½ c. chopped pecans
regular margarine	1 (6 oz.) pkg. semisweet
1 (7 oz.) jar marshmallow	chocolate pieces
creme	½ c. chopped pecans

Combine sugars, evaporated milk and butter in 3-qt. heavy saucepan. Cook over medium heat, stirring constantly, until mixture comes to a boil. Continue cooking to soft ball stage (234°), about 10 to 12 minutes. Remove from heat.

Blend in marshmallow creme and vanilla. Remove 2 c. of hot mixture to bowl. Add butterscotch pieces and ½ c. pecans. Stir until smooth. Pour into greased 9" square baking pan.

Add chocolate pieces and ½ c. pecans to remaining hot mixture. Stir until chocolate is melted and mixture is smooth. Spoon evenly over butterscotch layer and spread lightly with spatula to make even layer. Cover and refrigerate until firm. Cut into 1½" squares. Makes 36 pieces.

TWO-MINUTE MICROWAVE FUDGE

A very chocolatey fudge filled with creamy marshmallows. A California farm woman makes batches of this fudge for gift-giving during the holidays. "With this recipe, you really can make a lot of last-minute gifts in a hurry," she explained.

1 (1 lb.) box confectioners sugar, sifted	**¼ c. plus 1 tblsp. milk**
½ c. baking cocoa	**1 tblsp. vanilla**
½ c. butter or regular margarine	**½ c. chopped walnuts**
	1 c. miniature marshmallows

Combine all ingredients in 3-qt. glass mixing bowl. Microwave (high setting) 2 minutes. Stir until well blended. Pour into buttered 8" baking dish. Cover and refrigerate until set. Cut into 1" squares. Makes 64 pieces.

EASY BROWN SUGAR FUDGE

A Montana woman made this fudge the first year she was married and has been making it ever since. "It's so easy to make and never fails," she told us. "The brown sugar gives it a different flavor."

2 c. brown sugar, packed	**1 tsp. vanilla**
1 c. sugar	**1 (12 oz.) pkg. semisweet chocolate pieces**
1 c. evaporated milk	**1 c. chopped pecans**
½ c. butter or regular margarine	
1 (7 oz.) jar marshmallow creme	

Combine sugars, evaporated milk and butter in 3-qt. heavy saucepan. Cook over medium heat, stirring constantly, until mixture comes to a boil. Continue cooking until mixture reaches soft ball stage (234°), stirring occasionally. Remove from heat.

Add marshmallow creme and vanilla; stir until smooth. Add chocolate pieces and pecans; stir until chocolate is melted. Spread mixture in buttered 13x9x2" baking pan. Cover and refrigerate until firm. Cut into 1½" squares. Makes 48 pieces.

LAZY DAY FUDGE

Peanut butter fans will love this ultra-creamy fudge. Be sure to chill until ready to serve and return any leftovers to the refrigerator. Because of the cream cheese in the recipe, this fudge must not stand at room temperature for long.

1 (6 oz.) pkg. semisweet
   chocolate pieces
½ c. butter or
   regular margarine
¼ c. milk
1 tblsp. vanilla
	1 (1 lb.) box confectioners sugar
	1 c. cream-style peanut
	   butter
	1 (8 oz.) pkg. cream
	   cheese, softened

Combine chocolate pieces and butter in 2-qt. heavy saucepan. Cook over low heat until melted. Remove from heat. Stir in milk and vanilla.

Sift confectioners sugar into mixing bowl. Add peanut butter, cream cheese and chocolate mixture. Beat with electric mixer at medium speed until well blended and smooth. Turn into buttered 13x9x2" baking pan. Cover and refrigerate until firm. Cut into 1½" squares. Store in refrigerator. Makes 48 pieces.

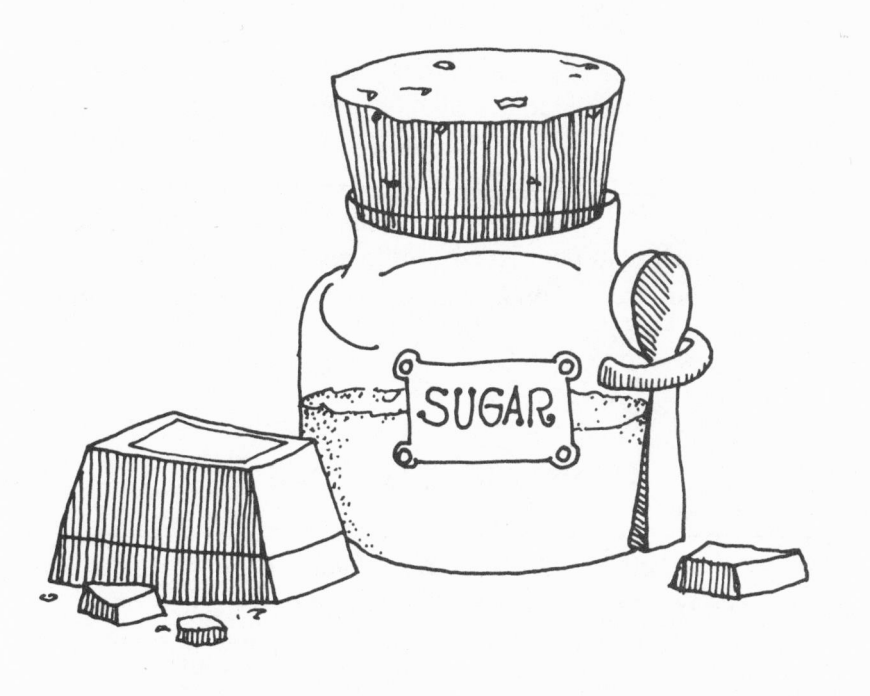

ROCKY ROAD FUDGE

A Utah farm woman turns to this recipe when she needs a last-minute candy to make for bake sales and bazaars. (See photo, Plate 4.) "It sells faster than I can put it onto plates," she wrote us.

**1 (10 oz.) pkg.
miniature marshmallows**
**2 (8 oz.) milk chocolate
candy bars**
**1 c. butter or
regular margarine**

4 c. sugar
**1 (13 oz.) can evaporated
milk**
2 c. chopped walnuts

Sprinkle one half of marshmallows in greased 13x9x2" baking pan. Refrigerate while preparing chocolate mixture.

196

Cut up chocolate bars and butter; place in large mixing bowl.

Combine sugar, evaporated milk and remaining marshmallows in 4-qt. heavy Dutch oven. Cook over medium heat, stirring constantly, until mixture comes to a boil. Continue cooking, stirring constantly, 6 more minutes. Pour hot mixture over chocolate and butter. Stir vigorously until chocolate and butter are melted and mixture begins to thicken. Stir in walnuts. Pour evenly over marshmallows. Cover and refrigerate until firm. Cut into pieces, about 1" square. Store in refrigerator. Makes 96 pieces.

QUICK POTATO FUDGE

Mild chocolate-flavored fudge—mashed potatoes make it extra smooth and creamy. "My sons really go for my fudge in a big way—one batch doesn't last long," said a New York farm wife.

3 (1 oz.) squares	**Dash of salt**
unsweetened chocolate	**1 (1 lb.) box confectioners**
3 tblsp. butter or	**sugar**
regular margarine	**1 to 2 tsp. milk**
⅓ c. unseasoned mashed	**Flaked coconut**
potatoes	**Chopped walnuts**
1 tsp. vanilla	

Melt chocolate and butter in saucepan over low heat. Remove from heat. Add mashed potatoes, vanilla and salt. Mix well.

Sift confectioners sugar into large bowl. Add chocolate mixture, mixing well. Mixture will be crumbly. Add 1 to 2 tsp. milk, if necessary, to make a mixture that can be kneaded.

Turn out on board and knead until smooth. Shape mixture into two rolls, 12" long and 1¼" in diameter. Roll in coconut or walnuts. Cut into ½" thick slices. Makes 48 pieces.

TRIPLE CHOCOLATE FUDGE

Three kinds of chocolate are blended into this quick and easy fudge. A Wisconsin woman has made over 100 batches for Christmas gifts since she received this recipe ten years ago.

4 c. sugar
1 (13 oz.) can evaporated
  milk
½ c. butter or
  regular margarine
2 (1 oz.) squares
  unsweetened chocolate

1 (10 oz.) pkg. miniature
  marshmallows
1 (12 oz.) pkg. semisweet
  chocolate pieces
1 (12 oz.) pkg. milk
  chocolate pieces
1 tsp. vanilla

Combine sugar, evaporated milk, butter and unsweetened chocolate in 5-qt. heavy Dutch oven. Cook over medium heat, stirring constantly, until mixture comes to a boil. Boil 8 minutes, stirring often. Remove from heat.

Stir in marshmallows, semisweet chocolate pieces, milk chocolate pieces and vanilla. Beat until smooth. Pour into buttered 15½x10½x1" jelly roll pan. Cool and cut into 1¼" squares. Makes 8 dozen pieces.

HEIRLOOM FUDGE

"My father's aunt owned a candy shop many years ago and this fudge recipe was her top seller," wrote a South Dakota farm woman.

"In fact," she continued, "this creamy candy recipe has been in our family for four generations."

2 c. sugar	¼ tsp. salt
¾ c. light cream	2 tblsp. butter or
2 (1 oz.) squares	regular margarine
unsweetened chocolate	½ tsp. vanilla
2 tsp. light corn syrup	

Combine sugar, light cream, chocolate, corn syrup and salt in 2-qt. heavy saucepan. Cook over medium heat, stirring constantly, until mixture boils. Cook to soft ball stage (234°) on candy thermometer without stirring. Remove from heat. Add butter. Cool to lukewarm (110°) without stirring.

Stir in vanilla. Beat until fudge stiffens and loses its gloss. Quickly turn into buttered 9x5x3" loaf pan. Score while still warm. Cool and cut into 1¼" squares. Makes 32 pieces.

7-MINUTE PECAN FUDGE

"My husband and father would be very disappointed if I didn't make this fudge during the holidays—it's the very best fudge, according to them," wrote a Kansas homemaker.

1 (4 oz.) pkg. chocolate	1 c. evaporated milk
pudding and pie filling	1 (12 oz.) pkg. semisweet
1 (3 oz.) pkg. vanilla	chocolate pieces
pudding and pie filling	2 c. miniature marshmallows
2 c. sugar	2 tsp. vanilla
3 tblsp. butter or	2 c. small pecan halves
regular margarine	

Combine chocolate pudding mix, vanilla pudding mix, sugar, butter and evaporated milk in 3-qt. heavy saucepan. Cook over medium heat, stirring constantly, until mixture comes to a boil. Boil 1 minute, stirring vigorously. Remove from heat.

Stir in chocolate pieces, marshmallows and vanilla. Beat with spoon until chocolate and marshmallows are melted. Add pecans and stir just until mixture loses its gloss. Pour into buttered 9" square baking pan. Spread evenly. Cool completely. Cut into 1" squares. Makes 36 pieces.

Mmm! What Good Candy!

Take a mental trip though a candy store as you riffle through this chapter and decide which confection you'd like to make first.

Looking for easy recipes to make in less than an hour? How about Chocolate Peanut Butter Bars, crunchy with graham crackers, peanut butter and semisweet chocolate pieces? Or, in 15 minutes you can turn out a batch of rich, buttery Chocolate Toffee or Chocolate Marshmallow Cups.

If you want to spend a little time and effort to make some absoutely spectactular candies, then make a batch of Chocolate-covered Cherries. The cherries are wrapped in an easy-to-make fondant and each one is lovingly dipped in a bath of melted chocolate. They are not difficult—just time consuming. But, they're worth every minute! And they make marvelous gifts.

At Eastertime, make your own Chocolate-covered Easter Eggs—they are so much better than what you can buy in the stores and your youngsters will feel very special.

For Christmas, try Chocolate Peanut Brittle. It's chock-full of peanuts and laced with rich chocolate flavor.

CHOCOLATE MINT HEARTS

Instead of a card on Valentine's Day, send your favorite person a box of these dainty, chocolate hearts with pale pink peppermint filling. A delicious way to say, "Won't you be my Valentine?"

1 (12 oz.) pkg. semisweet chocolate pieces	½ c. light corn syrup
¼ c. shortening	4½ c. sifted confectioners sugar
5 tblsp. butter or regular margarine	1 tsp. peppermint extract
	Red food color

Combine 1 c. of the chocolate pieces and 2 tblsp. of the shortening in top of double boiler. Melt over hot water. Spread evenly in aluminum foil-lined 15½x10½x1" jelly roll pan, using back of spoon. Chill in refrigerator until firm (about 20 minutes). Carefully invert onto waxed paper-lined baking sheet. Gently peel off foil. Return to refrigerator.

Combine butter, corn syrup and one half of confectioners sugar in large saucepan. Cook over medium heat, stirring constantly, until mixture comes to a full boil. Add remaining confectioners sugar, peppermint extract and a few drops of red food color; stir vigorously until well blended (about 3 minutes). Remove from heat.

Pour fondant onto greased baking sheet. Cool just long enough to handle (about 5 minutes). Knead until soft, about 2 minutes. Roll out fondant between two pieces of waxed paper to ⅛" thickness, making 15x10" rectangle. Remove top sheet of waxed paper. Carefully place fondant layer on chocolate layer. Remove second sheet of waxed paper. Chill 15 minutes.

Melt remaining chocolate pieces and 2 tblsp. shortening as before. Spread melted chocolate evenly over fondant layer. Chill 15 to 20 minutes. Cut into hearts or other desired shapes with cookie cutters. Chill until ready to serve. Makes 24 (2") hearts.

CHOCOLATE PEANUT BUTTER BARS

An Iowa farm woman was en route to California when she heard this recipe on the car radio. She hastily copied it on the road map and made it soon as she returned home. "My grandchildren love these bars as they taste real peanut-buttery and chocolatey," she wrote. (See photo, Plate 4.)

1 (1 lb.) box confectioners sugar	2½ c. graham cracker crumbs
1 c. butter or regular margarine	1 (6 oz.) pkg. semisweet chocolate pieces
1¼ c. crunch-style peanut butter	

Sift confectioners sugar into mixing bowl. Add butter and peanut butter. Beat with electric mixer at medium speed until light and creamy, about 2 minutes. Stir in graham cracker crumbs. Pat mixture into 13x9x2" baking pan.

Melt chocolate in top of double boiler over hot water. Spread over peanut butter layer. Let stand until chocolate sets. (Refrigerate, if necessary.) Cut into 1½x1" pieces. Makes 64 pieces.

CHOCOLATE-COVERED CHERRIES

"I make these deluxe Chocolate-Covered Cherries for all of the family birthdays. Our daughters insist that they taste 50 times better

than those that you buy in a candy store," wrote a Colorado woman. An elegant candy that would make an impressive gift. (See photo, Plate 1.) Our tasters begged us to make another batch.

⅓ c. soft butter or
    regular margarine
⅓ c. light corn syrup
½ tsp. vanilla
½ tsp. salt
3½ to 4 c. sifted
    confectioners sugar

1 (1 lb.) jar red mara-
    schino cherries with stems,
    well drained
2 (8 oz.) milk chocolate
    candy bars, cut up

Beat together butter, corn syrup and vanilla in mixing bowl until smooth, using electric mixer at medium speed. Gradually add salt and 3 c. of the confectioners sugar, mixing well. When mixture becomes too stiff to beat, stir with spoon. Add enough confectioners sugar to make a mixture that can be kneaded. Form mixture into 10" roll. Wrap in plastic wrap or waxed paper; refrigerate roll until firm.

Cut roll into 1" slices. Cut each slice into quarters. Flatten each piece in palm of hand; place a cherry in center. Fold up fondant around cherry until it is completely covered. Place on waxed paper-lined baking sheet. Chill until firm.

Melt milk chocolate in top of double boiler over hot water. Cool slightly. Dip fondant-covered cherries in chocolate; place on waxed paper-lined baking sheets. Refrigerate until chocolate sets. Store in refrigerator. Makes about 40 cherries.

CHOCOLATE PEANUT BUTTER BALLS

"I received this recipe from a busy farm wife who makes up large batches of these and freezes them for 4-H meetings. They make a big

hit with the kids," wrote a Nebraska farm wife. "My husband likes these even though he isn't crazy about peanut butter."

1 c. butter or regular margarine	1 (6 oz.) pkg. semisweet chocolate pieces
1¼ c. crunch-style peanut butter	½ (8 oz.) milk chocolate bar (4 oz.)
1 (1 lb.) box confectioners sugar, sifted	1 (2½x2½x½") piece paraffin wax, cut up
3½ c. toasted rice cereal	

Melt butter in 2-qt. heavy saucepan over low heat. Add peanut butter; stir until blended. Remove from heat.

Combine confectioners sugar and rice cereal in mixing bowl. Pour hot peanut butter mixture over all; mix thoroughly, using hands. Shape mixture into 1" balls. Place on waxed paper-lined baking sheet. Cover and refrigerate 1 hour.

Combine chocolate pieces, milk chocolate bar and paraffin in top of double boiler. Place over hot water until melted. Dip chilled peanut butter balls in chocolate mixture to coat. Place on waxed paper-lined baking sheets. Store in refrigerator. Makes 6 dozen pieces.

EASY PEANUT CLUSTERS

Homemade chocolate-covered peanuts with a hint of butterscotch. A Missouri homemaker created this original recipe because her family loves peanuts and chocolate. "When the candy jar is half-full, I make another batch of clusters so that the jar is never empty," she told us.

1 (12 oz.) pkg. semisweet
   chocolate pieces
1 (12 oz.) pkg. butterscotch
   flavored pieces

3 c. salted Spanish
   peanuts

Melt together chocolate and butterscotch pieces in top of double boiler over hot water. Stir until smooth. Stir in peanuts. Drop mixture by rounded teaspoonfuls onto waxed paper-lined baking sheets. Chill in refrigerator until set. Makes 54 clusters.

BUTTERSCOTCH/PEANUT BUTTER BARS

A candy that tastes very much like a popular commercial candy bar that's chewy and full of peanuts. A great favorite with youngsters and adults.

1 c. brown sugar, packed
⅔ c. butter or
   regular margarine
¼ c. dark corn syrup
¼ c. crunch-style
   peanut butter
1 tsp. vanilla
4 c. quick-cooking oats

1 (6 oz.) pkg. semisweet
   chocolate pieces
1 (6 oz.) pkg. butterscotch
   flavored pieces
⅔ c. crunch-style
   peanut butter
1 c. salted Spanish
   peanuts

Combine brown sugar, butter and corn syrup in 2-qt. heavy saucepan. Cook over medium heat until mixture is smooth. Add ¼ c. peanut butter and vanilla; stir until blended. Pour hot mixture over oats in bowl. Mix well. Press into greased 15½x10½x1" jelly roll pan.

Bake in 375° oven 12 minutes.

Meanwhile, melt chocolate pieces and butterscotch pieces in heavy saucepan over low heat. Add ⅔ c. peanut butter and peanuts, stirring to mix well. Spread over first layer when it is removed from oven. Cool on rack.

Refrigerate until firm. Cut into 2x1½" bars. Makes 48 pieces.

CHOCOLATE TOFFEE CANDY

Four ingredients and a few simple steps produce a rich, buttery toffee, crunchy with pecans. A Kansas farm wife calls this her favorite 15-minute homemade candy.

½ c. coarsely chopped
  pecans
½ c. butter or
  regular margarine

¾ c. brown sugar, packed
½ c. semisweet chocolate
  pieces

Sprinkle pecans in bottom of buttered 8" square baking pan.

Combine butter and brown sugar in 2-qt. heavy saucepan. Cook over medium heat, stirring constantly, until mixture comes to a boil. Continue cooking, stirring constantly, until mixture reaches hard crack stage (295°) on candy thermometer. Immediately pour hot mixture over pecans, spreading evenly. Sprinkle with chocolate pieces. Let stand 5 minutes. Spread melted chocolate evenly over all. When chocolate is set, break up into pieces. Makes about ¾ lb.

CHOCOLATE-COVERED EASTER EGGS

Once you have tried this recipe, we bet you'll never buy another Easter egg. These Easter eggs are very easy to make. Vary the pudding flavor to suit each youngster's taste. (See photo, Plate 1.)

½ c. butter or	1 tsp. vanilla
regular margarine	1 c. chopped walnuts
1 (5¼ oz.) pkg. chocolate	5 (1 oz.) squares
pudding and pie filling	unsweetened chocolate,
½ c. milk	melted and cooled
1 (1 lb.) box confectioners	20 miniature marshmallows
sugar, sifted	Assorted colored sugars

Melt butter in 3-qt. heavy saucepan. Stir in pudding mix; blend until smooth. Gradually stir in milk. Cook over medium heat, stirring constantly, until mixture is very thick and starts to boil. Cook until mixture leaves the sides of the pan. Remove from heat.

Stir in confectioners sugar and vanilla. Mix until smooth. Stir in walnuts. Cool until mixture is stiff enough to hold its shape.

Shape mixture into 12 eggs, using about 2 tblsp. for each. Place on waxed paper-lined baking sheet. Refrigerate 30 minutes. Dip each egg in cooled chocolate. Place on cooling rack over waxed paper. If you wish to decorate with marshmallow flowers, place on egg before chocolate sets.

To make flowers, cut miniature marshmallows in thirds crosswise. Dip cut side of each piece in colored sugar. Arrange 5 pieces sugared side up on each egg to resemble flowers. Let stand until chocolate sets.

Or decorate with pastel flowers using your favorite decorating frosting as we did in our photo. Store in refrigerator. Makes 12.

CHOCOLATE CLUSTERS

A nutritious candy that youngsters will love. A North Dakota farm wife suggests making a triple batch and freezing half to keep on hand for last-minute company or gift-giving.

1 (12 oz.) pkg. semisweet chocolate pieces	**½ c. flaked coconut**
	½ c. raisins
1 (3 oz.) can chow mein noodles	**1 c. peanuts**

Melt chocolate pieces in top of double boiler over hot water. Remove from heat. Cool to room temperature. Add chow mein noodles, coconut, raisins and peanuts; mix until evenly coated. Drop mixture by heaping teaspoonfuls onto waxed paper-lined baking sheets. Chill in refrigerator until set. Makes 36 pieces.

CHOCOLATE MARSHMALLOW CUPS

A great snacking candy to have on hand for all occasions. Only four ingredients are needed to make this delectable confection. (See photo, Plate 5.)

3 c. miniature marsh-
    mallows
	1 c. crunch-style
	    peanut butter

1 (12 oz.) pkg. semisweet
    chocolate pieces
	½ c. butter or
	    regular margarine

Place 4 marshmallows each in 48 paper-lined 1¾" muffin cups. Combine chocolate pieces, peanut butter and butter in 2-qt. heavy saucepan. Cook over low heat until melted and mixture is smooth. Remove from heat.

Spoon chocolate mixture over marshmallows. Cover and refrigerate until set. Store in refrigerator. Makes 48 pieces.

CHOCOLATE PEANUT BRITTLE

If you have friends who adore peanut brittle, then be sure to make a batch of this shiny brittle with a strong chocolate flavor and give as a gift. A unique and different candy. (See photo, Plate 1.)

2 c. sugar	1½ c. salted peanuts
1 c. light corn syrup	1 (6 oz.) pkg. semisweet
½ tsp. salt	chocolate pieces
½ c. water	½ tsp. vanilla
2 tblsp. butter or	
regular margarine	

Combine sugar, corn syrup, salt and water in 3-qt. heavy saucepan. Cook over low heat until sugar is dissolved, stirring constantly. Cover and boil 2 minutes. Uncover; cook without stirring until mixture reaches hard ball stage (252°) on candy thermometer. Add butter and salted peanuts. Continue cooking to hard crack stage (300°), stirring constantly to prevent sticking. Remove from heat.

Quickly stir in chocolate pieces and vanilla. Spread thinly on buttered baking sheet. Stretch and pull as thin as possible using two forks. Cool well. Break into pieces. Makes about 2 lbs.

PEANUT BUTTER CANDY SQUARES

A cross between a cookie and a candy, this is a quick and easy confection that even younger children can make. Nutritious, too, with oatmeal and peanut butter in the mixture. (See photo, Plate 1.)

2 c. quick-cooking oats	**1 tsp. vanilla**
1¼ c. sifted flour	**⅓ c. dark corn syrup**
1 c. brown sugar, packed	**½ c. crunch-style**
1 tsp. salt	**peanut butter**
½ tsp. baking soda	**1 (6 oz.) pkg. semisweet**
¾ c. butter or	**chocolate pieces**
regular margarine	

Combine oats, flour, brown sugar, salt and baking soda in large mixing bowl.

Melt butter in saucepan. Remove from heat. Stir in vanilla and corn syrup. Pour over oat mixture; mix well. Press mixture in bottom of greased 13x9x2" baking pan.

Bake in 350° oven 20 minutes or until golden brown.

Spoon peanut butter over hot candy. Sprinkle with chocolate

pieces. Let stand 5 minutes. Spread mixtures over candy making swirls. Cool completely. Cut into 2" squares. Makes 24 pieces.

OLD-FASHIONED BUTTER CRUNCH

An Ohio woman has lost count of the number of times she has copied her butter crunch recipe for friends and neighbors. One of our faithful candy testers emphatically declared that this is the greatest candy recipe she's ever tasted.

1 c. butter or	2 tblsp. water
regular margarine	2 c. finely chopped
1¼ c. sugar	toasted almonds
2 tblsp. light corn	1 (6 oz.) pkg. semisweet
syrup	chocolate pieces

Melt butter in 3-qt. heavy saucepan over low heat. Add sugar, corn syrup and water. Cook over medium heat, stirring constantly, until mixture reaches hard crack stage (300°) on candy thermometer. Remove from heat. Stir in toasted almonds. Spread mixture in buttered 13x9x2" baking pan. Let stand 5 minutes. Sprinkle with chocolate pieces. When chocolate is melted, spread evenly over candy. Let cool completely. When chocolate is set, break up into pieces. Makes about 1¼ lbs.

CHOCOLATE CANDY ROLL

"This recipe would appeal to any 'chocolate freak'," wrote a Washington farm woman when she entered her Chocolate Candy Roll in a recipe contest. It was a grand prize winner.

½ c. butter or
   regular margarine
2 (1 oz.) squares
   unsweetened chocolate
1½ c. sifted confectioners
   sugar

1 egg, beaten
1 c. coarsely chopped
   pecans
4 c. miniature marsh-
   mallows
1 (3½ oz.) can flaked coconut

Melt together butter and chocolate in 3-qt. heavy saucepan over low heat. Remove from heat. Cool slightly.

Stir in confectioners sugar and egg; blend well. Then stir in pecans and marshmallows; mix until well coated. Divide mixture in half. Shape each into 12" roll. Carefully roll in coconut. Wrap in plastic wrap or waxed paper. Freeze. To serve, thaw and cut into ½" slices. Makes 48 pieces.

MINIATURE CANDY BARS

"A recipe given to me by a dear friend," wrote an Iowa farm woman. "My family thinks it is super and the kids ask me to make that 'little candy bar' for their birthdays." (See photo, Plate 1.)

1 (1 lb.) box confectioners
   sugar
⅔ c. sweetened
   condensed milk (not
   evaporated)
½ tsp. vanilla
½ tsp. almond extract

1 (12 oz.) pkg. semisweet
   chocolate pieces
1 (12 oz.) pkg. butterscotch
   flavored pieces
1 lb. chopped Spanish
   peanuts

Combine confectioners sugar, sweetened condensed milk, vanilla and almond extract in large bowl. Mix thoroughly, using hands to knead. Roll mixture between two sheets of plastic wrap to form

13x9" rectangle. Chill in refrigerator.

Meanwhile, melt chocolate and butterscotch pieces in top of double boiler over hot water. Stir in peanuts. Spread one half of chocolate mixture in buttered 13x9x2" baking pan.

Carefully place fondant layer on top. Spread remaining chocolate mixture on top. Refrigerate until firm.

Remove from refrigerator 10 minutes before cutting. Cut into 2x1½" bars. Store in refrigerator. Makes 48 pieces.

CHOCOLATE COCONUT BARS

A tried and true family favorite from Nebraska. A three-layer mini candy bar. Crunchy graham cracker base, rich moist coconut center glazed with velvety smooth chocolate. You simply can't stop at one piece, so don't try.

2 c. graham cracker crumbs
½ c. sugar
½ c. melted butter or regular margarine
2 c. flaked coconut

1 (14 oz.) can sweetened condensed milk (not evaporated)
1 (6 oz.) pkg. semisweet chocolate pieces
1 tblsp. peanut butter

Combine graham cracker crumbs, sugar and butter in bowl; mix well. Press mixture in 13x9x2" baking pan.

Bake in 350° oven 10 minutes.

Meanwhile, combine coconut and sweetened condensed milk in bowl. Mix well. Spread over baked layer.

Bake in 350° oven 15 more minutes. Cool in pan on rack. Melt chocolate pieces and peanut butter in top of double boiler over hot water. Spread chocolate mixture over bars. Cut into 3¼x1⅛" bars. Makes 32 pieces.

CHOCOLATE-DIPPED
COCONUT BALLS

If you need a candy recipe that makes a big batch and takes little effort to make, do try these tiny coconut balls with little chocolate caps. (See photo, Plate 4.) Makes a handsome gift.

2 (1 lb.) boxes confectioners
    sugar
½ c. melted butter
    or regular margarine
1 (14 oz.) can sweetened
    condensed milk (not
    evaporated)

2 c. flaked coconut
1 (6 oz.) pkg. semisweet
    chocolate pieces
1 (2½x1¼x½") piece paraffin
    wax, cut up

Combine confectioners sugar, butter, sweetened condensed milk and coconut in bowl. Mix well. Shape mixture into 1" balls. Place on baking sheet. Freeze until firm.

Melt together chocolate pieces and paraffin wax in top of double boiler over hot water. Dip tops of frozen coconut balls, in warm chocolate mixture. (Chocolate will set immediately.) Store in cool place. Makes 8½ dozen pieces.

EASY TOFFEE BARS

An absolutely fabulous candy! Tastes and looks like butter crunch. And it all starts with a little soda cracker. Your friends will never guess the basic ingredient.

35 soda crackers	1 c. brown sugar, packed
with unsalted tops	1 (6 oz.) pkg. semisweet
1 c. butter or	chocolate pieces
regular margarine	

Lightly grease 15½x10½x1" jelly roll pan. Line bottom of pan evenly with crackers.

Combine butter and brown sugar in 2-qt. heavy saucepan. Cook over medium heat, stirring constantly, until mixture comes to a boil. Continue cooking 3 more minutes, stirring constantly. Pour mixture evenly over crackers.

Bake in 375° oven 15 minutes. Remove from oven. Sprinkle with chocolate pieces. Let stand 5 minutes. Spread melted chocolate over crackers. While still warm, cut between crackers making 35 squares. Chill in refrigerator until set. Makes 35 pieces.

Index

A

Angel Food Cake, Chocolate, 61
Aunt Georgie's Chocolate Cake, 17

B

Banana Fudge Cookies, 77
Banana Split Dessert, 171
Basic Chocolate Layer Cake, 38
Bavarian Mint Pie, 141
Black Magic Cake, 24
Black Walnut/Chocolate Cookies, 98
Blonde Brownies, 115
Browned Butter Frosting, 68, 102
Brownie(s), 101-128
  Blonde, 115
  with Browned Butter Frosting, 102
  Buttermilk, 119
  Caramel Chocolate Squares, 123
  Chewy Coconut-Cherry, 127
  Chewy Fudge, 106
  Chocolate Chip, 116
  Chocolate Coconut, 124
  Chocolate Cream Cheese, 112
  Chocolate Marbled, 103
  Chocolate Peppermint Bars, 107
  Coffee Iced, 121
  Cupcakes, Light Chocolate, 74
  Double Boiler, 111
  Easy Chocolate, 120
  Fingers, Deluxe, 109
  Friendship, 110
  German Chocolate/Cheese, 117
  Mississippi Mud Bars, 114
  Mix, Homemade, 104

  1949, 125
  Pecan, 109
  Pudding, 125
  Rich Peppermint, 127
  Rocky Road Bars, 105
  Semisweet Chocolate, 118
  Sticks, Chocolate, 122
  Toasted Marshmallow, 121
  Tri-level, 113
  Twirl Baked Alaska, 172
  Walnut Drops, 76
Butter Cream Frosting, 19
Butter Crust, 150
Buttermilk Brownie Sheet Cake, 49
Buttermilk Brownies, 119
Buttermilk Frosting, 49
Butterscotch Fudge, Chocolate, 189
Butterscotch/Peanut Butter Bars, 206

C

Cacao, 11
  Bean(s), 8, 10
    Harvesting of, 10
    Roasting of, 11
  Hook, 10
  Tree, 9, 10
Cake(s), 15-74
  Angel Food, Chocolate, 61
  Aunt Georgie's Chocolate, 17
  Black Magic, 24
  Chocolate Cream, 55
  Chocolate Pecan Sponge, 60
  Chocolate Sauerkraut, 27
  Chocolate/Vinegar, 52

Cupcakes
    with Browned Butter Frosting,
        Chocolate, 68
    with Chocolate Glaze,
        Chocolate, 64
    Coconut Cream-filled Choco-
        late, 69
    Creme-filled Chocolate, 67
    Light Chocolate Brownie, 74
    with Maple Frosting, Fudge,
        65
    Mocha-filled Chocolate, 71
    with Peanut Butter Frosting,
        Chocolate, 66
    Pineapple/Chocolate, 72
    Toll House, 70
    Quick and Easy, 73
Elegant Chocolate Log, 62
Layer
    Basic Chocolate, 38
    Chocolate Chiffon, 32
    Chocolate-Lemon, 45
    Chocolate/Lemon, 37
    Chocolate Velvet, 46
    Cream Cheese/Chocolate, 41
    Delightful Apricot/Fudge, 44
    Deluxe Chocolate, 40
    Egyptian Chocolate, 34
    Grandma's Chocolate, 31
    Mile-high Chocolate, 35
    Old World Chocolate, 33
    Prize-winning Chocolate, 42
    Sour Cream/Chocolate, 30
    Whimsical Chocolate Birth-
        day, 28
Magic Chocolate Swirl, 56
Marachino Cherry/Chocolate, 51
Mayonnaise Chocolate, 23
Mexican Chocolate, 58
Mocha Chiffon, 57
Moist Chocolate Loaf, 53
Mouth-watering Chocolate, 19

Outstanding Chocolate, 20
Pumpkin/Chocolate, 54
Red Beet Chocolate, 26
Sheet
    Buttermilk Brownie, 49
    with Cocoa/Nut Frosting,
        Chocolate, 50
    Speedy Chocolate, 48
Southern Pound, 61
Spiced Chocolate/Applesauce,
    16
Victory Chocolate, 20
West Haven Chocolate, 18
Whole Wheat Chocolate, 22
Zucchini/Chocolate, 25
California Cream Fudge, 186
Candy(ies) 201-216
    Bars, Miniature, 213
    Butterscotch/Peanut Butter Bars,
        206
    Chocolate Clusters, 209
    Chocolate Coconut Bars, 214
    Chocolate-covered Cherries, 203
    Chocolate-covered Easter Eggs,
        208
    Chocolate-dipped Coconut Balls,
        215
    Chocolate Marshmallow Cups,
        210
    Chocolate Mint Hearts, 202
    Chocolate Peanut Brittle, 210
    Chocolate Peanut Butter Balls,
        204
    Chocolate Peanut Butter Bars,
        203
    Chocolate Toffee Candy, 207
    Easy Peanut Clusters, 205
    Easy Toffee Bars, 215
    Old-fashioned Butter Crunch,
        212
    Roll, Chocolate, 212
    Squares, Peanut Butter, 211
Caramel Chocolate Squares, 123

Caribbean Fudge Pie, 154
Cheese Pie, Chocolate, 150
Cherries, Chocolate-covered, 203
Cherry Drops, Chocolate/, 76
Cherry Pie, Chocolate, 153
Chess Pie, Chocolate, 147
Chewy Chocolate Squares, 95
Chewy Coconut-Cherry Bownies, 127
Chewy Fudge Brownies, 106
Chewy Fudge Sauce, 181
Chocolate, *see also* Brownies, Cakes, Candies, Cookies, Desserts, Frostings, Fudge, Pies and Sauces
    Baking, 12
    Bloom, 14
    Conching, 9
    how to make Curls, 14
    Cutouts, 29, 41
    how to Grate, 14
    History of, 8
    Liquid Baking, 12
    Liquor, 11
    Manufacture of, 11
    how to Melt, 13
    Milk, 9, 11, 12
    Pieces, Semisweet, 12
    Premelted Baking, 12
    Products, 12
    Semisweet, 12
    how to Store, 14
    Substitutes, 13
    Sweet cooking, 12
    Syrup, 12
    Tips on Cooking, 13
    Unsweetened, 12
    White, 13
Chocolatl, 8
Choco-Mint Snaps, 99
Choco-Nut Pie, Creamy, 138
Cinnamon Whipped Cream, 35
Cocoa
    Baking, 13
    Breakfast, 11
    Butter, 9, 11

    /Butter Filling, 38
    Cake, 11
    Frosting, 22, 80, 115
    Icing, 36
    Instant, 13
    /Nut Frosting, 50
    Powder, 11
    Press, 9
    Sweet Milk, 11
Coconut Balls, Chocolate-dipped, 215
Coconut Bars, Chocolate, 214
Coconut Brownies, Chocolate, 124
Coconut/Chocolate Nut Drops, 90
Coconut Cream-filled Chocolate Cupcakes, 69
Confectioners Sugar Glaze, 51, 55, 60
Cookies, 75-100
    Bars
        Butter Pecan Chocolate, 92
        Chewy Chocolate Squares, 95
        Chocolate Chip Pizza, 93
        Chocolate Lebkuchen, 90
        Peanut Butter Fudge, 94
        Toll House, 91
    Drop
        Banana Fudge, 77
        Brownie Walnut, 76
        Chocolate/Cherry, 76
        Chocolate Marshmallow, 79
        Chocolate Mincemeat Jumbles, 85
        Chocolate Sandwich, 82
        Chocolate Saucepan, 80
        Chocolate/Walnut Kisses, 84
        Coconut/Chocolate Nut, 90
        Cottage Cheese/Chocolate, 86
        Devil's Food, 87
        Frosted Chocolate, 78
        Nutritious Chocolate, 84
        Raisin/Chocolate, 89
        Triple Chocolate, 81
        Whole Wheat/Raisin, 88
    Molded
        Chocolate Linder, 97

Choco-Mint Snaps, 99
Refrigerated
    Black Walnut/Chocolate, 98
    Chocolate, 100
Rolled
    Chocolate Mint Creams, 96
Cortez, Hernando, 8
Cottage Cheese/Chocolate
    Cookies, 86
Cream Puffs, Chocolate-filled, 165
Creamy Chocolate Frosting, 27
Creamy Chocolate Pie, 143
Creamy Choco-Nut Pie, 138
Creamy Coffee Frosting, 47
Creme-filled Chocolate Cupcakes,
    67

D

Dark Chocolate Icing, 31
Dark Chocolate Pudding, 177
Delightful Apricot/Fudge Cake, 44
Deluxe Brownie Fingers, 109
Deluxe Chocolate Layer Cake, 40
Dessert(s), 157-184
    Banana Split, 171
    Bread Pudding, Chocolate, 159
    Bread Pudding, Layered Choco-
        late, 163
    Brownie Twirl Baked Alaska, 172
    Chocolate Almond Swirl, 174
    Chocolate Charlotte Russe, 169
    Chocolate Cream Jelly, 166
    Chocolate Peppermint Frozen,
        175
    Chocolate Rum Tortoni, 176
    Chocolate Torte Royale, 167
    Chocolate-filled Cream Puffs,
        165
    Easy Chocolate Fondue, 178
    Frozen Fudge Pops, 170
    Hot Fudge Pudding Cake, 161
    Neapolitan, 173
    Peppermint Chocolate Mousse,
        168

Pudding, Dark Chocolate, 177
Pudding, Milk Chocolate, 177
Pudding, Pompadour, 158
Pudding, Steamed Chocolate,
    160
Souffle, Cold Chocolate, 164
Souffle, Hot Cocoa, 162
Devil's Food Cookies, 87
Divine Triple Chocolate Pie, 133
Double Boiler Brownies, 111
Double Chocolate Fudge, 186
Double Fudge Brownie Pie, 152

E

Easy Brown Sugar Fudge, 194
Easy Chocolate Brownies, 120
Easy Chocolate Fondue, 178
Easy Chocolate Frosting, 104
Easy Peanut Clusters, 205
Easy Toffee Bars, 215
Egyptian Chocolate Cake, 34
Elegant Chocolate Log, 62
English Chocolate Houses, 9

F

Favorite Family Fudge, 191
Ferdinand V, King, 8
Filling(s)
    Chocolate, 166
    Chocolate/Cheese, 44
    Cocoa/Butter, 38
    Marshmallow, 83
    Mint Cream, 96
    Sweetened Cream, 45
    Vanilla Creme, 67
Fluffy Chocolate Frosting, 23
Fluffy Chocolate Pie, 139
Fluffy Frosting, 59
Foamy Sauce, 163
Fondue, Easy Chocolate, 178

French Chocolate Fudge, 190
French Chocolate Pie, 136
Friendship Brownies, 110
Frosted Chocolate Drop Cookies,
    78
Frosting(s), *see also* Glazes, Icings
    and Fillings
  Browned Butter, 68, 102
  Butter Cream, 19
  Buttermilk, 49
  Chocolate, 79
  Chocolate Cream Cheese, 106
  Chocolate Fluff, 16
  Chocolate-Lemon, 46
  Chocolate 7-Minute, 39
  Cinnamon Whipped Cream, 35
  Cocoa, 22, 80, 115
  Cocoa/Nut, 50
  Creamy Chocolate, 27
  Creamy Coffee, 47
  Easy Chocolate, 104
  Fluffy, 59
  Fluffy Chocolate, 23
  Fudge, 110, 114
  Hundred Dollar, 24
  Maple, 66
  Milk Chocolate, 119
  Mocha/Chocolate, 52
  Mocha Fluff, 41, 72
  Peanut Butter, 66
  Peppermint, 128
  Pineapple, 73
  Seafoam, 29
  Semisweet Chocolate, 120
  Sour Cream/Chocolate, 30
  Sweetened Whipped Cream, 34
  Vanilla Cream, 32
  Whipped Chocolate, 21
Frozen Chocolate Cream Pie, 156
Frozen Fudge Pops, 170
Frozen Peppermint Chocolate Pie,
    155

Fudge, 185-200
  Bars, Peanut Butter, 94
  Brownie Pie, Double, 152
  Brownies, Chewy, 106
  Cake, Delightful Apricot/, 44
  California Cream, 186
  Chocolate Butterscotch, 189
  Chocolate Wonder, 192
  Cookies, Banana, 77
  Cupcakes with Maple Frosting,
    65
  Double Chocolate, 186
  Easy Brown Sugar, 194
  Favorite Family, 191
  French Chocolate, 190
  Frosting, 110, 114
  Heirloom, 198
  Lazy Day, 195
  Marshmallow, 189
  Mother's Cocoa, 187
  /Pecan Topping, 183
  Peppermint Sauce, Hot, 183
  Pie, Caribbean, 154
  Pops, Frozen, 170
  Quick Potato, 197
  Rocky Road, 196
  Sauce, Chewy, 181
  Sauce, Peanut Butter, 180
  Sauce, Very Thick, 182
  7-Minute Pecan, 199
  Triple Chocolate, 198
  Two-minute Microwave, 194
  Two-tone, 193
  Velvet Chocolate, 188
Fudgy Chocolate Sauce, 178

G

German Chocolate/Cheese
  Brownies, 117
German Chocolate Mallow Pie, 140
German Chocolate Pie, 154
German Sweet Chocolate Pie, 146

Glaze(s)
    Chocolate, 64, 166
    Coffee, 58
    Confectioners Sugar, 55, 60
    Pecan/Chocolate, 48
    Satiny Chocolate, 56
    Shiny Chocolate, 70, 97
Grandma's Chocolate Layer Cake, 31

H
Hard Sauce, 161
Heirloom Fudge, 198
Homemade Brownie Mix, 104
Honey Chocolate Sauce, 180
Hot Cocoa Souffle, 162
Hot Fudge Peppermint Sauce, 183
Hot Fudge Pudding Cake, 161
Hundred Dollar Frosting, 24

I
Icing(s)
    Chocolate, 67, 87
    Cocoa, 36
    Coffee, 121
    Coffee/Chocolate, 81
    Confectioners Sugar, 51
    Dark Chocolate, 31

L
Layered Chocolate Bread Pudding, 163
Lazy Day Fudge, 195
Lebkuchen, Chocolate, 90
Lemon Cake, Chocolate-, 45
Lemon Frosting, Chocolate-, 46
Lemon Layer Cake, Chocolate/, 37
Light Chocolate Brownie Cupcakes, 74
Log, Elegant Chocolate, 62

M
Maple Frosting, 66
Maraschino Cherry/Chocolate Cake, 51
Marbled Chocolate Rum Pie, 131
Marshmallow Brownies, Toasted, 121
Marshmallow Cookies, Chocolate, 79
Marshmallow Cups, Chocolate, 210
Marshmallow Filling, 83
Marshmallow Fudge, 189
Marshmallow Pie, Chocolate/, 134
Mayonnaise Chocolate Cake, 23
Meringue Shell, 130, 137, 168
Mile-high Chocolate Cake, 35
Milk Chocolate Frosting, 119
Milk Chocolate Fudge Topping, 12
Milk Chocolate Pie, 147
Milk Chocolate Pudding, 177
Miniature Candy Bars, 213
Mint Cream Filling, 97
Mint Creams, Chocolate, 96
Mint Pie, Bavarian, 141
Mint Snaps, Choco-, 99
Mississippi Mud Bars, 114
Mocha/Chocolate Frosting, 52
Mocha-filled Chocolate Cupcakes, 71
Mocha Fluff Frosting, 41, 72
Moist Chocolate Loaf, 53
Mom's Chocolate Sauce, 181
Montezuma, 8
Mother's Chocolate Fudge, 187
Mouth-watering Chocolate Cake, 19

N
Neapolitan Dessert, 173
1949 Brownies, 125
Nutritious Chocolate Drops, 84

O

Old-fashioned Butter Crunch, 212
Old World Chocolate Cake, 33
Outstanding Chocolate Cake, 20

P

Peanut Brittle, Chocolate, 210
Peanut Clusters, Easy, 205
Peanut Butter Balls, Chocolate, 204
Peanut Butter Bars, Butterscotch/, 206
Peanut Butter Bars, Chocolate, 203
Peanut Butter Candy Squares, 211
Peanut Butter Frosting, 66
Peanut Butter Fudge Bars, 94
Peanut Butter Fudge Sauce, 180
Pecan Brownies, 109
Pecan Chocolate Bars, Butter, 92
Pecan/Chocolate Glaze, 48
Pecan Pie, Chocolate, 148
Pecan Pie Crust, 132
Pecan Sponge Cake, Chocolate, 60
Pecan Topping, Fudge/, 183
Peppermint Bars, Chocolate, 107
Peppermint Brownies, Rich, 127
Peppermint Chocolate Mousse, 168
Peppermint Chocolate Pie, Frozen, 155
Peppermint Frosting, 128
Peppermint Frozen Dessert, Chocolate, 175
Peppermint Hearts, Chocolate, 202
Peppermint Sauce, Hot Fudge, 183
Peter, Daniel, 9
Pie(s), 129-156
　Bavarian Mint, 141
　Caribbean Fudge, 154
　Chocolate Angel, 130
　Chocolate Cheese, 150
　Chocolate Cherry, 153

Chocolate Chess, 147
Chocolate Chiffon, 135
Chocolate Macaroon Cream, 145
Chocolate/Marshmallow, 134
Chocolate Nut Toffee, 151
Chocolate Orange Meringue, 137
Chocolate Pecan, 148
Chocolate Ripple, 149
Chocolate Rum, 142
Creamy Chocolate, 143
Creamy Choco-Nut, 138
Divine Triple Chocolate, 133
Double Fudge Brownie, 152
Fluffy Chocolate, 139
French Chocolate, 136
Frozen Chocolate Cream, 156
Frozen Peppermint Chocolate, 155
German Chocolate, 154
German Chocolate Mallow, 140
German Sweet Chocolate, 146
Marbled Chocolate Rum, 131
Milk Chocolate, 147
Rich Chocolate, 144
Two-layer Chocolate, 132
Pie Crust(s)
　Butter, 150
　Chocolate, 134
　Chocolate Graham, 151
　Pecan, 132
　Vanilla Wafer, 141
Pineapple/Chocolate Cupcakes, 72
Pineapple Frosting, 73
Pompadour Pudding, 158
Prize-winning Chocolate Cake, 42
Pumpkin/Chocolate Cake, 54

Q

Quick and Easy Chocolate Cupcakes, 73
Quick Potato Fudge, 197

INDEX

R

Raisin/Chocolate Cookies, 89
Raisin Cookies, Whole Wheat/, 88
Red Beet Chocolate Cake, 26
Rich Chocolate Pie, 144
Rich Peppermint Brownies, 127
Ripple Pie, Chocolate, 149
Rocky Road Bars, 105
Rocky Road Fudge, 196
Rum Pie, Chocolate, 142
Rum Pie, Marbled Chocolate, 131
Rum Tortoni, Chocolate, 176

S

Sauce(s)
 Chewy Fudge, 181
 Chocolate Syrup, 184
 Foamy, 163
 Fudge/Pecan Topping, 183
 Fudgy Chocolate, 178
 Hard, 161
 Honey Chocolate, 180
 Hot Fudge Peppermint, 183
 Mom's Chocolate Sauce, 181
 Peanut Butter Fudge, 180
 Very Thick Fudge, 182
Sauerkraut Cake, Chocolate, 27
Seafoam Frosting, 29
Semisweet Chocolate Brownies, 118
Semisweet Chocolate Frosting, 120
7-Minute Pecan Fudge, 199
Shiny Chocolate Glaze, 70, 97
Sour Cream/Chocolate Frosting, 30
Sour Cream/Chocolate Layer Cake, 30
Southern Pound Cake, 61
Speedy Chocolate Sheet Cake, 48
Steamed Chocolate Pudding, 160
Sweetened Cream Filling, 45
Sweetened Whipped Cream, 34

T

Toasted Marshmallow Brownies, 121
Toffee, 152
Toffee Bars, Easy, 215
Toffee Candy, Chocolate, 207
Toll House Bar Cookies, 91
Toll House Cupcakes, 70
Topping, Chocolate/Nut, 71
Tortoni, Chocolate Rum, 176
Tri-level Brownies, 113
Triple Chocolate Cookies, 81
Triple Chocolate Fudge, 198
Two-layer Chocolate Pie, 132
Two-minute Microwave Fudge, 194
Two-tone Fudge, 193

V

Vanilla Cream Frosting, 32
Vanilla Creme Filling, 67
Vanilla Wafer Crust, 141
Velvet Chocolate Fudge, 188
Victory Chocolate Cake, 20
Vinegar Cake, Chocolate/, 52

W

Walnut Drops, Brownie, 76
Walnut Kisses, Chocolate/, 84
West Haven Chocolate Cake, 18
Whimsical Chocolate Birthday Cake, 28
Whipped Chocolate Frosting, 21
White Chocolate, 13
Whole Wheat Chocolate Cake, 22
Whole Wheat/Raisin Cookies, 88

Z

Zucchini/Chocolate Cake, 25